The Obelisks of
WARWICKSHIRE

The Obelisks of
WARWICKSHIRE

BREWIN BOOKS

First published by
Brewin Books Ltd, 56 Alcester Road,
Studley, Warwickshire B80 7LG in 2013
www.brewinbooks.com

ISBN: 978-1-85858-515-4

A Cataloguing in Publication Record
for this title is available from the British Library.

Typeset in Adobe Garamond Pro
Printed in Great Britain by
Cambrian Printers.

CONTENTS

ST LAWRENCE :
NAPTON

INSCRIPTION :
THE PARISHIONERS OF NAPTON /
HAVE ERECTED THIS / MONUMENT /
TO THE GLORY OF GOD / AND IN THE
MEMORY OF THOSE MEN / OF THE
VILLAGE WHO GAVE / THEIR LIVES /
FOR THEIR COUNTRY DURING / THE
GREAT WAR / 1914 - 1919 / GREATER
LOVE HATH NO MAN / THAN THIS
THAT A MAN LAY DOWN / HIS
LIFE FOR HIS FRIENDS /
ST JOHN XV 13 V

Preface

Why a book about Warwickshire's obelisks? The Warwickshire Gardens Trust promotes the conservation of gardens and parkland in the historic county and, equally, seeks to raise public awareness of related subjects as part of its educational purpose. This book – part guide, part history – is in the latter category.

In 2005, following the publication of Richard Barnes's excellent *The Obelisk: a Monumental Feature in Britain,* the Trust decided to embark on a project to survey and find out more about the obelisks of the historic county, with a view to publication. A group of volunteers set out on an enjoyable and eye-opening round of inspections, followed by research, discussion, further finds and second visits before assembling this guide.

Finding these intriguing monuments will take you to some of the less-visited but no less interesting parts of the county. Sites are indicated on the small maps, and there is a county map showing general locations. Bus and train services, access and parking arrangements should be checked; they were correct at the time of going to press.

Obelisk in honour of Edward Willes, Jephson Gardens, Royal Leamington Spa, 1875.

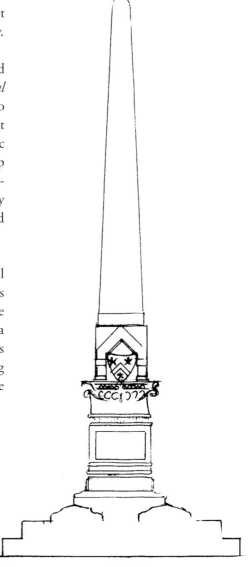

Foreword

This is an unusual and a most worthwhile production, a survey of memorials lovingly undertaken over the last seven years by four friends of twenty years standing. Non-denominational and aesthetic, each obelisk, its facture and its subject is described and categorised by size. Medium is the height of a small house. Large indicates a gigantic tuning fork by which the viewer may calibrate the scale of the landscape or the city from far away. Unlike on one's mantelpiece or in some great continental garden they don't in this country tend to come in pairs, that is of course with the exception of the monumental tombs of the sixteenth century, where they have lasted well and one of which furnishes the earliest example in this elegant guide.

Edmund Fairfax-Lucy
President, Warwickshire Gardens Trust

The Charlecote connection – a view to the obelisk on Welcombe Bank, three miles distant. PHOTO: David P Howard

What is an obelisk?

A true obelisk on the ancient Egyptian model is a shaft of stone, more or less square in cross-section, tapering upwards and ending in a small pyramid: the pyramidion.

Four Warwickshire obelisks,
of different sizes and proportions,
approximately to the same scale,
with estimated heights:

LEFT to RIGHT
Priors Hardwick War Memorial, 7 feet
St Mary's War Memorial, Leamington, 14 feet
Hoo Hill, Polesworth, 21 feet
Umberslade, 70 feet

pyramidion

shaft of obelisk

cornice

pedestal

plinth, often stepped

base

Materials

GRANITE
left to right: pink-brown, grey, black-green

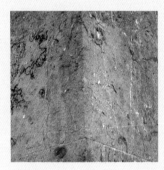 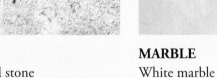

LIMESTONE
left: Hornton stone; right: Portland stone

MARBLE
White marble

SANDSTONE
left: pink, with lichen; right: buff, with bedding planes.

BRONZE

Egypt and Rome

Obelisks first appeared at Heliopolis, the centre of a cult of sun-worship in ancient Egypt about 5,000 years ago. An obelisk would have been raised by a king in honour of the sun god. The most significant part was the pyramidion, whose pyramidal form had symbolic meanings. Obelisks were polished, sheathed in gold or electrum (an alloy of gold and silver) and incised with hieroglyphics. Touching the sky, they blazed with the reflected sun and represented the relationship between the god and the king. The faces of the shaft, inscribed with religious texts, were like the rays of the sun – the word of god coming down to the earth. Obelisks were usually associated with altars in open solar temples, or in pairs to flank the entrance to a temple, sanctifying the space.

They were quarried in one piece, usually from granite but also from basalt and hard limestone. All granite obelisks came from a quarry in the Lybian mountains at Aswan, on the east bank of the Nile below the First Cataract. One lies there now, abandoned when cracks appeared. Evidence suggests that after three sides were carved and decorated, the fourth was probably quarried by inserting wooden wedges into holes; when soaked they expanded and split the granite. Thousands of men would lever the obelisk out, drag it down to the Nile and on to a barge towed by rows of boats during the annual flooding of the river. One theory suggests that on arrival at Heliopolis or Karnak the obelisk was dragged base first up a ramp until it toppled over into a socket carved in the bedrock; this and its low centre of gravity giving it great stability. Thus obelisks sprang directly from the ground, their appearance reinforcing the idea that they were the sun's rays descending from the sky.

An obelisk abandoned unfinished in the quarry at Aswan.
PHOTO: Dan Lundberg / flickr.com

By the time that the Romans occupied Egypt, taking over from the Greeks, the worship of the goddess Isis and her consort Osiris was widespread. The Romans revered the Egyptian gods as more ancient than their own and established a cult of Isis in Europe. They transported Egyptian obelisks to Rome and re-erected them to sanctify sites associated with the worship of Isis. After the fall of the empire some obelisks were demolished or used for stone. Some remained standing; others lay where they fell or sank into marshy ground.

A pyramidion reflects the sun – imagine it gilded!

LEFT: *Hieroglyphics and the reflected sun on an obelisk at Luxor, Egypt.*
PHOTO: Tona & Yo / flickr.com

Obelisks could be thought of as descending from the heavens as well as ascending from the earth.

RIGHT: *The one remaining obelisk at Heliopolis in the late nineteenth century, from a scrapbook by William Vaugn Tupper.*
PHOTO: Boston Public Library, Boston, USA / flickr.com

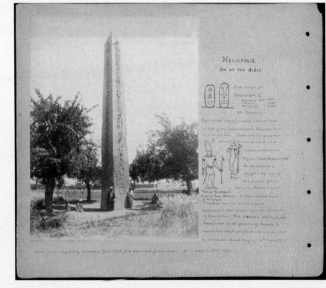

The Renaissance and after

From the 10th century people showed increasing interest in the historical remains of Rome. Egyptian elements began to appear in the work of artists: a medal produced around 1438 was one of the first to depict an obelisk. Following the sack of Constantinople in 1453 scholars and books found their way to the west. Texts from third and fourth century Alexandria led to a belief that Christian doctrine had its roots in ancient Egyptian religion. With increasing knowledge of the ancient world there developed the powerful conviction that all knowledge, all skills and all basic architectural wisdom had come from Egypt. This explains why successive popes and their architects re-erected fallen obelisks and remodelled the city's public spaces around existing obelisks. Pius II (1458-64) made a start, but under Sixtus V (1585-90) architects produced and began to implement a master-plan for Rome dominated by obelisks. In later years they became the centrepieces of civic spaces and the focal points of vistas, aggrandising the city as the undisputed centre of Christendom. Visitors to Rome were impressed. Some

The obelisk in the Piazza del Popolo was the first to be removed from Egypt to Rome. It was set up in the Circus Maximus in 10 BC. Under Pope Sixtus V it was reassembled and re-erected in 1589. PHOTO: Berthold Werner / commons.wikimedia.org

who saw the obelisks would take a new interest in the history, philosophies, religions and architecture of ancient Greece and Rome as well as Egypt.

The obelisk came to be seen as an element of classical architecture. Initially, sculptors and masons who were commissioned to produce tombs had substituted classical elements for gothic. Obelisks replaced gothic finials. Later, through a simple association with a mythical ancient Rome, they came to symbolize eternity. This was not their significance in ancient Egypt itself, nor were small obelisks associated with Italian funerary art.

In northern Europe from the mid-sixteenth century small obelisks became a feature of church tombs, printed frontispieces, decorative arches and gardens. The first known use of obelisks in England was in 1575 for the Privy Garden at Kenilworth Castle (see page 15). A marble obelisk of between 20 and 30 feet in height was erected in the gardens of the Palace of Nonsuch, Surrey, but demolished in 1682. Obelisks were used to ornament roofs and parapets at Hardwick Hall, Derbyshire, and Montacute House, Somerset, both in the 1590s. In architecture, particularly in the Netherlands, northern Germany and England, obelisks may also have signalled Catholicism where it was suppressed, or support for philosophies that traced their origins to Egypt.

In Britain church tombs could be rich three-dimensional monuments that exhibited the motifs of strapwork, obelisks, columns, canopies, heraldry, armour and busts of the deceased. A typical example is the monument to Robert Dudley and his wife in the Beauchamp Chapel of St Mary's Church, Warwick. Such constructions were increasingly criticized for taking up space intended for worship, as well as for their eclectic style. In response, people who wanted to assert their status were commemorated in mural monuments although they might be buried under the floor of the church or outside. Urns, inscriptions, sculpted figures and other elements were arranged in a typically triangular composition, piled up against a background slab in the form of a broad obelisk. Such memorials occur in huge numbers in Europe. British churches have some of the finest; they appeared until a relatively late date. The memorial to Sir Thomas Foley in Great Witley Church (page 14) and to the Archer family in the parish church of Tanworth-in-Arden (page 21) are atmospheric examples. Many were executed by immigrant Flemish Protestant sculptors although the form was derived from Bernini's baroque papal tombs in Rome. Bernini also undertook the re-erection of obelisks in Roman gardens and in the Fountain of the Four Rivers for papal clients. Egypt began to be visited by scholars and explorers, notably from France, who brought back more reliable accounts of Egyptian antiquities. Much attention was devoted to deciphering hieroglyphics, without success. There was a trade in mummies, which were pulverized for use by apothecaries.

ABOVE: *Obelisks as architectural ornaments at Montacute House, Somerset.*
PHOTO: Les Mildon / geograph.org.uk

ABOVE: *Obelisk on the tomb of Robert Dudley, Earl of Leicester (died 1588) and his wife Lettice in the Beauchamp Chapel, St Mary's Church, Warwick.*

RIGHT: *The magnificent obeliskal memorial to Sir Thomas Foley (died 1733) in Great Witley Church, Worcestershire. This form of church monument derived from Renaissance models and was common throughout Europe.*
PHOTO: P.L. Chadwick / geograph.org.uk

Kenilworth Castle Garden
1575, reconstructed 2008

Size: Small
Material: Painted wood
Location & access: Castle Green, Kenilworth
English Heritage make an admission charge
Bus: Stagecoach services 12, X17, X18 (Sun)
Nearest rail stations: Coventry, Leamington Spa
Parking: Car park at the Brays,
off Castle Road

Map contains Ordnance Survey Data © Crown copyright and database 2011, 2012.

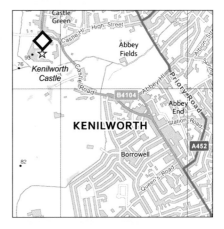

From the Middle Ages to the Civil War in the seventeenth century Kenilworth Castle was a formidable defensive stronghold of strategic importance. The Norman castle built in the 1120s was enlarged, strengthened and improved by John of Gaunt, fit for a royal palace. Inherited by his son Henry IV it was owned by the monarchy until the 1640s. Early in 1553 John Dudley, Duke of Northumberland was given Kenilworth Castle but in August 1553 he was executed for plotting to install his daughter-in-law Lady Jane Grey on the throne. Kenilworth and Warwick Castles returned to the monarchy.

It was not until Elizabeth I became Queen in 1558 that the Dudley sons, Ambrose and Robert, prospered. In 1561 Ambrose was made Earl of Warwick and given Warwick Castle. Robert became the Queen's favourite and Master of the Horse, organised her progresses and accompanied her on her favourite pastime, hunting. He was given Kenilworth Castle in 1563 and created Earl of Leicester and Baron of Denbigh.

Queen Elizabeth spent the summer months progressing through the countryside "to show herself to the people". She visited Kenilworth Castle in 1566, 1568 and 1572, when Dudley built 'Leicester's Building' to accommodate the Queen and her retinue. For the visit in 1575 he added a tower with a staircase for her private use.

By the 1570s Robert was falling out of favour with the Queen and was unpopular with the people as rumours spread about his wife, Amy Robsart, and her fatal fall down stairs. In 1575, still hoping to marry Elizabeth, he made extraordinary preparations to entertain her with theatricals, music, dancing, hunting and most sensational of all, a new garden in the latest Italian fashion on the site of the old "pleasance, covered with fine grass containing most beautiful, homely and sweet-scented flowers". The new ideas came from his contacts on the continent, travellers who visited Rome and the gardens of the Villa d'Este and the Villa Lante, and his patronage of the Italian artist Federigo Zuccaro, who painted portraits of the Queen and himself while visiting London and Kenilworth Castle early in 1575. The idea of the garden was to remind the Queen of his power and prestige, his noble ancestry, his education and his knowledge of Rome, classical and republican with symbolic Italianate artefacts.

The site of the one-acre garden is ten feet below the castle wall but within the outside wall. The problem of access was resolved by a terrace with a balustrade decorated with small obelisks, spheres and white bears. Steps from an arbour at each end led down into the garden, laid out in two halves, a fountain of white Carrara marble from Tuscany in the centre and an aviary on the north side. The two halves were divided into four, each with two obelisks on the central path. The pierced obelisks, fifteen feet tall, standing on four balls as a pedestal, were described as porphyry, a rare purple Egyptian marble, but were probably painted wood, as they are today in the recent reconstruction by English Heritage. They represented glory and immortality and revealed Dudley's knowledge of classical Rome and Renaissance ideology. The ten-inch orb on top represented the rational and civilised side of man's nature. The whole obelisk was the apex of spiritual attainment. The Kenilworth Castle Privy Garden terrace and the obelisks were the first to be used in a garden in England.

Pierced and painted wooden obelisks in the restored Elizabethan gardens at Kenilworth Castle. PHOTO: Egghead06 / commons.wikimedia.org

The Eighteenth Century

In Britain many landowners at the beginning of the century had walled gardens and grounds around their houses with formal deer parks beyond. Many sought to make their estates more suitable for fox-hunting and carriage drives and more productive of crops, livestock and timber, at the same time demonstrating how cultured they were. The new look of classical or rustic buildings in an informal verdant landscape was inspired by the paintings of Poussin and Claude Lorrain, and the experience of Rome and Italian gardens which landowners would have visited on the Grand Tour. The architects Nicholas Hawksmoor and John Vanburgh set a high standard with the landscape of Castle Howard in Yorkshire. It included an obelisk 100 feet tall, built in 1714 and a thrilling event in the landscape. Landowners everywhere had their estates remodelled by fashionable landscape gardeners. In Warwickshire in the mid-century obelisks were erected as 'eyecatchers' – focal points in the landscape – at Farnborough Hall and Umberslade Hall as well as at Wroxton House in neighbouring Oxfordshire in 1741. Some eighteenth-century obelisks commemorated people and families or celebrated events. The models were the Roman acquisitions from Egypt as re-erected by the Renaissance popes, sometimes with added plinths and sculpture.

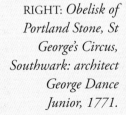

LEFT: *100-foot obelisk at the crest of the Stray, Castle Howard, Yorkshire: architect Nicholas Hawksmoor, 1714.*
PHOTO: Pauline Eccles / geograph.org.uk

RIGHT: *Obelisk of Portland Stone, St George's Circus, Southwark: architect George Dance Junior, 1771.*

2 Farnborough
1740s

Size: Large
Material: Limestone
Location: At the end of the half-mile terrace south of Farnborough Hall, a National Trust property
Bus: To Farnborough by Stagecoach service 77 between Leamington & Avon Dassett; Johnson's Excel bus 277 between Banbury & Lighthorne Heath
Nearest rail station: Banbury
Access & parking: Signed from A423

Map contains Ordnance Survey Data © Crown copyright and database 2011, 2012.

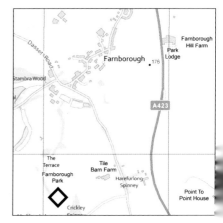

The Farnborough estate in south Warwickshire was acquired by Ambrose Holbech in 1684, but it was his son William Holbech who reconstructed the old manor house and resided there from 1692 until his death in 1717. His son William II, after a prolonged Grand Tour returned in 1734 to remodel the hall and embark on an ambitious project to build a great terrace on the ridge running from the house with a slight incline and curve for three quarters of a mile in a southerly direction.

By the mid-eighteenth century the landscape movement was gathering pace. Across the valley lived Sanderson Miller (1716-1780), a friend of William Holbech and architect of the ruined tower at Hagley and the tower at Edgehill. Architectural features were an essential element of landscaped parks; Farnborough has an Ionic temple and an oval pavilion. Ahead on a promontory stands a tall, slender, elegant obelisk built by William Hiorne of Warwick: "One of the most magnificent obelisks erected as a visual accent." To the south the view is across the valley to Warmington; to the west, Edgehill and the site of a historic battle.

The design of the landscape cannot be attributed with certainty to either Holbech or Miller; most likely it was a collaboration between friends. Timothy Mowl calls it innovative: "It represents that aesthetic shift from an inward-looking, shrubbery-shaded eclecticism around the skirts of a house to a visual embracing of the wider landscape." There is a story in the family that the obelisk was not put there as the end of a walk but to mark a meeting point. William's brother lived at the main house (which is no longer there) in Mollington. The obelisk was the halfway point between the two houses. The brother never laid out his terrace but if the escarpments are followed round towards Mollington Wood there are the foundations of another temple beyond the obelisk.

In 1742 John Loveday the antiquary recorded in his journal that he "rode on Mr. W. Holbech's terrace". An unknown visitor mentioned the obelisk in 1746 but the date on the pedestal is 1751, perhaps marking the final completion of work on the terrace. In 1756 Bishop Pococke having returned from his travels in Egypt and the Near East started a tour of England, stayed at Radway and visited Farnborough. He wrote in his journal: "He has made a very grand grass terrace winding round the hill for half a mile ... there is an obelisk at the end which may be 80 feet high."

It is difficult building such a slender obelisk with blocks of limestone. In 1823 it collapsed and was then rebuilt in its original form in 1828. In 1896 the Reverend George Miller, grandson of Sanderson Miller, in his book *Rambles round the Edge Hills* described it as a "handsome, well-proportioned obelisk".

During World War Two Farnborough was an auxiliary military hospital. It was then that the names of Italian prisoners were cut on the pedestal, the only names on it.

The well-proportioned obelisk draws the visitor to the end of the terrace, where the view opens out on to the wider landscape.

3 Umberslade
1749

Size: Large
Material: Limestone ashlar
Access: Permissive access via stile opposite Obelisk Farm, Pound House Lane. Avoid damage to crops
Bus: Johnson's X20 to Hockley Heath from Birmingham or Stratford
Flexibus 517 between Redditch & Wootton Wawen
Nearest rail stations: Dorridge, Wood End
Parking: Lanes and bridges over M40, with care. Do not obstruct farm traffic and accesses

Map contains Ordnance Survey Data © Crown copyright and database 2011, 2012.

Anyone who travels the M40 regularly will have seen this near the junction with the M42. It stands in a field on Obelisk Farm, Nuthurst Hill, south of Hockley Heath. This quiet corner of the countryside seems remote from the noise and rush of the motorway.

It is a slender spike over 70 feet high, built of limestone blocks. If it ever bore an inscription it is concealed by the mass of ivy around its base. It is surmounted by a golden ball that originally supported an eight-armed cross. Construction began in 1748, at the behest of Thomas Archer of Umberslade Hall, and was completed in 1749. The builder was William Hiorne of Warwick, assisted by local labour.

It was sited so as to be seen from Umberslade Hall, which was only completed around 1700, as a focal point in the landscaped park. Sadly, this relationship is obscured by a modern screen of conifers, probably planted to hide the motorway from the hall. The siting is entirely in the tradition of the English Landscape movement whereby eighteenth-century and later landowners ornamented their parks with architectural features. Thomas Archer's architect uncle, also Thomas, was probably the designer of the mural memorial to Andrew Archer in the form of an obelisk in Tanworth-in-Arden parish church.

The symbolic golden ball that sometimes surmounted obelisks from the Renaissance onwards would also have reflected the sun from any angle. Baron Archer's addition of an eight-armed cross was also in the tradition of the popes who similarly Christianised the ancient Egyptian obelisks which they re-erected in Rome. William Shenstone and Lady Luxborough, the county's arbiters of taste, tut-tutted about the propriety of the cross and the size of the obelisk, but only in the context of its role as a landscape feature and nothing more.

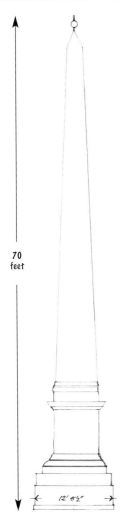

70 feet

12' 5½"

On a knoll characteristic of the Arden landscape, the obelisk can be seen from many viewpoints. It was sited so as to be seen from Umberslade Hall.

BELOW: *Memorial to the Archer family in Tanworth-in-Arden parish church.*

The Nineteenth Century

The legacy of the eighteenth century was a number of obelisks so prominent that they entered public consciousness. The obelisk became a means of commemorating worthy people. As the Victorian era progresses a visual trend is evident: the handsome proportions of the Roman monuments are altered for modest private memorials. Obelisks get smaller while pedestals become bigger, creating space for inscriptions to a number of departed family members.

Egypt and its antiquities were never out of the public eye for long, starting perhaps with Britain's ousting of the French after the Battle of the Nile in 1798. Napoleon retreated but left his archaeologists behind to continue their studies. 'Mummy Mania' peaked around 1825. The French successfully transported an obelisk from Luxor to France: it was erected in the Place de la Concorde and unveiled in 1836. Recollections of the exploit prompted thoughts of retrieving Cleopatra's Needle, the fallen Alexandrian obelisk that had been given to the British Government in 1820.

The sculptor John Bell (1811-1895), an enthusiast for obelisks, had a plan to display Cleopatra's Needle at the 1851 Great Exhibition in Hyde Park, but it did not come to fruition. However, a number of obelisks were exhibited as examples of manufacture and would have been seen by thousands of people during the six months of the exhibition. A more lasting exposure was at the Crystal Palace on Sydenham Hill from 1854 – a replica of the monument proposed for the cemetery at Scutari, Constantinople, in honour of the British troops who died in the Crimean War, 1854-56. Seen by millions of people it may have established the association between obelisks and commemorating the dead. There is a story of a visitor to Leamington who asked a new taxi driver to take him to the cemetery, only to be delivered to the gates of Jephson Gardens where the Willes obelisk among gloomy evergreens lent the gardens a funereal air. Scutari had no aesthetic influence; the designs for memorials offered by monumental masons were practical and affordable, handsome at best.

Bell proposed a big obelisk in Hyde Park in honour of Prince Albert following the success of the Great Exhibition and its transfer to Sydenham. Victoria and Albert viewed designs in 1858 but Albert died in 1861; his memory was honoured by the Albert Memorial. Cleopatra's Needle again became an object of public attention in the 1870s. Its journey from Alexandria became a three-year saga that was followed in every detail by the newspapers before it was unveiled on London's Embankment in 1878.

In Warwickshire, two prominent obelisks commemorate notable people: the soldier-adventurer-journalist Fred Burnaby in St Philip's Churchyard, Birmingham; and Mark Philips at Welcombe Bank. Lesser-known monuments have their own stories: Mr Buck of the Oddfellows, also at St Philip's, and the memorial to Lt-Col. Miller on the slopes of Edge Hill.

Erecting Cleopatra's Needle on the Thames Embankment, 1878.
© Illustrated London News Ltd/Mary Evans Picture Library

Cemeteries

Even before the nineteenth century many churchyards were overcrowded and insanitary. Private companies laid out non-denominational cemeteries from 1819. An example is Key Hill, Hockley, Birmingham, opened in 1836. Following the Public Health Acts of the midcentury new public burial grounds were laid out by local authorities. Many obelisks may be seen in the big cemeteries at London Road in Coventry and Witton in Birmingham. As a non-Christian monument the obelisk served other beliefs. Some obelisks were Christianised; sometimes their severity was softened. Older cemeteries may be enjoyed for their distinctive memorials, noble trees and peaceful character. Warstone Lane cemetery; Handsworth cemetery; the churchyard of St Mary's, Handsworth; South Yardley cemetery; Lodge Hill and Brandwood End cemeteries, all in Birmingham, are also worth exploring. Elsewhere, Evesham Road, Stratford-upon-Avon; Brunswick Street in Leamington; Birmingham Road in Warwick; and Rectory Road in Sutton Coldfield are of equal interest.

CLOCKWISE FROM LEFT:
Key Hill Cemetery, Hockley, Birmingham, opened in 1836 as the Birmingham General Cemetery.

Obeliskal headstone and other memorials in London Road Cemetery, Coventry, designed by Joseph Paxton and opened in 1848. There are more than thirty obelisks in the older part of the cemetery.

Jewish Cemetery, Witton.

ABOVE: *The Anglican chapel, Witton.*

LEFT: *Two styles of obelisk from the pre-First World War catalogue of memorial designs by G L Taylor, "Est. 1868, Stone, Marble & Monumental Masons, Gosford Bridge, Coventry". The left-hand design is similar to the war memorials at Hurley, Napton and Wormleighton.*
Coventry History Centre

4 Compton Verney
1848

Size: Small
Material: White Cornish granite
Location: Grounds of Compton Verney, roughly southeast of the house towards the lake
Bus: Johnson's Excelbus/Stagecoach Service 269 between Stratford-upon-Avon and Banbury
Nearest rail station: Stratford-upon-Avon
Parking: Car park off the B4086 between Wellesbourne and Kineton
Access: Charges payable for car park and admission

Map contains Ordnance Survey Data © Crown copyright and database 2011, 2012.

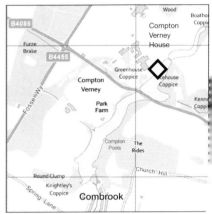

The obelisk by the lake at Compton Verney marks the site of the original family chapel. The history of it goes back to 1086 when the Benedictines built the church for the village known as Compton Murdak, between the manor and the village houses, probably on both sides of the brook. During the Middle Ages, the agrarian changes and social unrest aggravated by the Black Death caused the desertion of many villages in south Warwickshire, Compton Murdak among them, leaving just the church and the manor house.

In 1430 John Verney, through his connections with the Earl of Warwick, bought Compton Murdak for his brother Richard which, with later additions, became the Compton Verney estate. By 1522 the church was virtually the family chapel with the founding of a chantry and a family burial vault.

An engraving of Wenceslas Hollar's drawing of the Stuart house dated 1655, shows the medieval Benedictine chapel close to the house overlooking a mill pond created by damming the brook by the road.

The first alterations to the house and grounds were made by George Verney, 12th Baron Willoughby de Broke (1661-1728) who inherited Compton Verney in 1711, in the baroque style of avenues, canals and formal gardens just as it was becoming unfashionable. In 1741 the 14th Baron inherited Compton Verney and, through marriage, the neighbouring Chesterton. The extra income encouraged him to embark on further remodelling of the house with the architect Robert Adam from 1762-68.

RIGHT: *The obelisk is a scaled-down replica of the Lateran obelisk at Rome – the likely model for the Farnborough, Umberslade, Fiennes Miller and Frederick Burnaby obelisks.*

A stone slab in front of the obelisk (not erected until 1848) is inscribed:

Under this stone is the entrance into the Vault Belonging to the Verney Family they continued to Bury here till the Old Chapel was taken down in the Year 1772. The Vault extends from beneath Eastwards as on the North side of This stone the Chapel stood (the foundations of which are still Remaining) Under which many of the Family are Buried besides Those in the Vault none of whom were remov'd. This stone was left for the information of Posterity That they might not ignorantly Dig into or Remove the Ground here Planted Upon.

ABOVE: *Compton Verney from the bridge. The obelisk is among the trees, left.*
PHOTO: Ruth Sharville / geograph.org.uk, reproduced by kind permission of the Compton Verney House Trust

The grounds were landscaped from 1769-1780 by Capability Brown in the new, natural style of grass, trees and water, uniting the ponds into an extensive lake. In 1772 he demolished the old chapel to improve the view of the lake from the house and also the view of the house from the new bridge. The late medieval Verney tomb and other memorials were moved to the new chapel but the underground burials were left in the old family vault. Two of the yews from the old churchyard are still standing.

In the 1840s the 16th Baron Willoughby de Broke considered *"putting up an obelisk to mark the tomb of my Ancestor whos mortal remains lie in the Old Family Vault under the Cypresses in the Clump. Hugh Williams says Cornish Porphyry NB apply to Mr. Tyfry at Foweyey large obelisk Q the proper size – I don't know what to say to all this. Gowans is going to dig over the old Clump and level it. The Cypresses will look very handsome"*.

The connection between Willoughby de Broke and Mr Treffry was George Lucy of Charlecote, an M.P. for Fowey. For twenty years Treffry corresponded with Lucy, looked after his property in Fowey and supported his election campaigns, until the Reform Act of 1832. In 1834 Mr Treffry and his mother were invited to Charlecote for Christmas.

A basal inscription on the obelisk records: *"This obelisk is an exact model of the Lateran obelisk at Rome. The granite was given by Joseph Thomas Teffry Esq of Place in Cornwall."* In the Shakespeare Birthplace Trust Records Office there is a framed drawing with an inscription on the back *"This drawing is the obelisk from the late Mr. Tyfry of Place Fowey Cornwall made of white Cornish granite. The drawing is from a plate in the Montfaucon antiquities after the Lateran obelisk of Rome from which plate this obelisk was named and I erected it over the old family vault near the Upper Pool at Compton about four years ago (1848) Sept 19 1852 Henry Lord Willoughby de Brook in his 80th year."*

Mr Treffry (1782-1850) was an important man in Cornwall, an industrialist in tin and copper mining; china clay and granite quarrying; canal, tramway and railway building with his own harbour at Par. The high-quality white granite was quarried five miles inland to the east of Luxulyan valley. Exploitation on a large scale depended on transport. It was Mr Treffry who cut the two-mile canal from Ponts Mill to Par in the 1830s. In 1842 the Par Tramway over the Treffry ten-arched granite viaduct enabled blocks of granite, after rough cutting and dressing, to be moved down the valley to Ponts Mill where they were offloaded by crane on to the canal boats to Par harbour. There the final dressing was carried out on the Granite Quay before a heavy crane lifted them into the hold of a vessel, a schooner or a ketch. Often the destination was London. Did the obelisk travel by ship to London and then by canal or railway to the Midlands?

The methods used to extract the granite were not so different from the way the obelisks were quarried in Egypt when Tuthmosis III (1504-1450 BC) celebrated his jubilee by erecting nine obelisks. The largest surviving one is the Lateran obelisk in Rome.

5 Fiennes Miller
Edgehill 1854

Size: Medium
Material: Hornton stone, also known as Marlstone Rock
Location: Private land north of Edgehill village and southeast of Radway. The site can be seen from public footpaths and from Radway village
Bus: Service 269 between Stratford-upon-Avon and Banbury
Nearest rail station: Banbury
Parking: in the villages, considerately

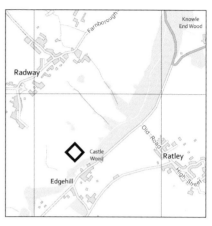

Map contains Ordnance Survey Data © Crown copyright and database 2011, 2012.

The obelisk on the former Radway Grange estate is situated on a grassy platform to the north of Edgehill Tower (now the Castle Inn) in the village of Edgehill. Edge Hill is an outlier of the Cotswolds, rising to about 700 feet (213 metres) above the valley. From the tower and public footpaths there are outstanding views to north and west, towards the village of Radway below and the spreading vale beyond: a magical spot. This is the inscription:

THIS OBELISK WAS ERECTED BY
CHARLES CHAMBERS ESQ^RE R.N.
IN 1854 TO COMMEMORATE THE
BATTLE OF WATERLOO,
WHERE THE VITH INNISKILLING DRAGOONS
WERE COMMANDED BY
LIEUT. COL. F. S. MILLER
WHO FOR HIS GALLANT CONDUCT
DURING THE ACTION IN WHICH HE WAS
VERY SEVERELY WOUNDED,
WAS MADE A COMPANION OF THE MOST
HONOURABLE ORDER OF THE BATH.

It raises questions: who was Charles Chambers? Why 1854, when the Battle of Waterloo was fought in 1815? What was Miller's gallant conduct in the battle?

Radway Grange and the estate were bought in 1712 by Sanderson Miller (senior) of Banbury, and enlarged by his son, the Sanderson Miller who contributed to the landscaping at Farnborough. He was responsible for building Edgehill tower and its associated mock ruins to mark the spot where in 1642 King Charles had raised his standard prior to the Battle of Edgehill at the start of the Civil War. Miller brought in an act of enclosure for the parish of Radway in 1756, and also landscaped the hillside above the Grange. One of his first landscaping projects on coming into his inheritance following the death of his father in 1737, was to harness the spring water coming off the hill near the summit. He made a fountain and cascade to flow down the hillside, and at the top he excavated a small pool to act as a reservoir, the soil being formed into a mound on the downhill side. The mound acted both as an ornamental feature and also as a retaining dam for the water. It was on this spot that the nineteenth century obelisk was sited.

In time the estate duly passed to Miller's son, Francis Sanderson (d.1818), and then to his grandson Fiennes Sanderson Miller. In 1812, then with the rank of Major, he was Superintendent of the Regimental School of the 6th Inniskilling Dragoons at Ballinaslo, Ireland, where the heavy cavalry regiment had been based for many years. In the early summer of 1815 the forces of Great Britain and Ireland were assembling in what is now Belgium for the confrontation with the French under Napoleon Bonaparte. The Inniskillings joined other regiments to form the Union Brigade under Sir William Ponsonby. Major Miller was promoted to the temporary rank of Lieutenant Colonel and commanded one of three squadrons, each of about 140 troopers.

At Waterloo on the 18th of June the heavy cavalry fought in two actions which brought about the defeat of the French. In the first, the light cavalry having failed to break the formation of the French infantry, the heavy cavalry charged from short range and butchered them. In five minutes Napoleon lost 5,000 men. Nearly all the guns belonging to the French attack were put out of action for the rest of the day. "Never in the annals of modern warfare has a cavalry charge been more decisive." It may be deduced that Miller led the charge, his fellow squadron commanders, Captains Madox and Browne, having been severely disabled in battle. Miller suffered two lance wounds and was pulled off his horse in the midst of the enemy's column. Other commanders had their horses killed under them. In the evening the Brigade, greatly reduced in numbers, supported the infantry "in the hottest part of the battle", exposed to the murderous French artillery. They eventually repulsed the French cavalry, who greatly outnumbered them, but at high cost to life and limb. Miller was carried off – one of his thighs was shattered by a 'canister shot'. From copies of letters to him we know that he was still recovering in Brussels in

ABOVE and RIGHT:
The obelisk on its platform encircled by ancient trees. It was sited so as to be seen from Radway Grange.

Reproduced by kind permission of the owner.

March 1816, long after the Inniskillings had returned to England, where they were fêted as the deciding force at Waterloo.

Charles Chambers and Fiennes Miller were cousins by marriage, as well as friends and neighbours in Radway and district. As a naval surgeon Chambers had been mentioned in despatches for his conduct during a hostile engagement with Russian ships in the Gulf of Finland. It is possible that Chambers attended Miller in Brussels, if only because there are no copies of letters from Charles to Fiennes – he didn't need to write to his cousin because he was with him.

In 1854 it was in Miller's honour that the obelisk was erected over his grandfather's pool, proudly overlooking the estate, Radway Grange and the plain beyond. It may have been occasioned by Chambers' approaching death; he died on 6th August 1854, aged 70. Linking both their names, it is as much a memorial to a generous man as it is to his gallant cousin. The obelisk is built in the local ironstone, the stone most likely being taken from the quarry in the village of Edgehill. Around the obelisk are several ancient lime trees, which probably date from the time of the original formation of the pool and cascades. Fiennes Sanderson Miller died in 1862, aged 83.

6 Hoo Hill
Polesworth 1850s?

Material: Hard sandstone
Size: Medium
Location: Private land 3/4 mile (1.1km) ESE of town
Access: Gate on the south side of the B5000 Grendon Road. Take great care!
Car park: Abbey Green Park off Grendon Road near the river bridge
Bus: Daily services from Tamworth or Nuneaton
Nearest rail station: Polesworth, limited service

Map contains Ordnance Survey Data © Crown copyright and database 2011, 2012.

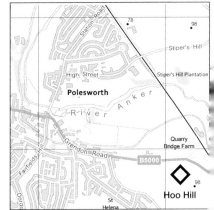

The site is a commanding one, overlooking Polesworth and the interweaving of the Grendon Road, the Coventry Canal, the West Coast main railway line and the River Anker where they squeeze between Hoo Hill and Stipershill. *Hoo* is an old word, the same as *hoe, howe* and *heugh,* meaning a spur of land or "a height enduring abruptly or steeply" – as may be appreciated from the canal towpath. From Grendon Road the obelisk is an eyecatcher, standing on the brow of the hill. The inscription reads: SITE OF THE CHAPEL OF ST LEONARD AT HOO / DEMOLISHED 1538 / 30TH HENRY VIII. A brick base supports three brown sandstone steps, surmounted by a steeper step, a cuboid pedestal, and the obelisk itself, all of blackened stone. The masonry is chipped; bricks poke out of the ground.

The story goes that during construction of the Trent Valley Railway between Rugby and Stafford in 1847 workmen excavating the Sandyways cutting uncovered skeletons and gravestones. They were thought to reveal the burial ground of the Norman chapel, and thus the site of the chapel itself, demolished during the suppression of the monasteries in the thirtieth year of Henry's reign. When the railway was widened, it is said, the obelisk was moved to its present site for safety reasons.

It is most likely to have been commissioned in the 1850s or early 1860s by the landowner, Sir George Chetwynd of Grendon Hall, perhaps at the suggestion of the Reverend John Duff Schomberg, incumbent of Polesworth from around 1840 to 1864. He had noted in the burial register the deaths of railway excavators through accident and disease. He visited the Great Exhibition in 1851 and may have seen obelisks there. In 1853 he noted a report of the 70-foot red stone obelisk erected to the memory of those who fell at the battle of Chillianwalla, India.

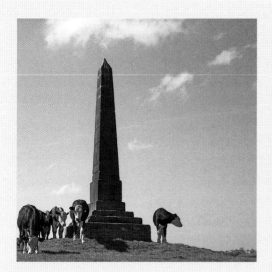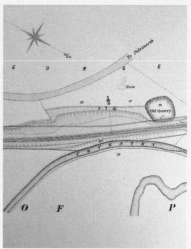

LEFT: *The blackened, battered obelisk on Hoo Hill overlooking the ancient town of Polesworth.* Reproduced by kind permission of the owner.

RIGHT: *No sign of an obelisk near the railway in a detailed survey of 1880. From the top it shows the Grendon Road over Hoo Hill, railway land in green, the Coventry Canal and the River Anker in the valley. The ruin was of Hoo Hill Barn, not the Norman chapel.* The National Archives, ref. RAIL 410/2118 part 2.

Recent studies for the county's Historic Environment Record show that in Norman times the chapel was the centrepiece of an area called Wood Park, granted to the Earl of Tamworth and intended to attract moneyed pilgrims bound for Polesworth Abbey. As a subsidiary chapel it would not have had a burial ground. It is more likely that remains found in 1847 were of much earlier date. It is believed that in this strategic location there was an Iron Age hill fort that was destroyed by nineteenth-century sand and gravel quarrying: another name for Hoo Hill was Gravel Pit Hill. No mention of human remains being uncovered has been found in correspondence from the building of the railway, nor any record of their re-interment. Schomberg's successor, the energetic Reverend Madan noted the obelisk in its present position probably at the beginning of his incumbency, 1866, confirmed by the first Ordnance Survey map, surveyed in 1883. This stretch of railway was not widened until around 1904.

The old quarry was probably filled with household rubbish in the late 1950s by Atherstone Rural District Council but incompletely capped. Judging by the damage to the obelisk it may have been dismantled to allow test drilling for coal by the National Coal Board in 1965. In the event the site was not opencast mined and there is a report of the opencast company re-erecting and refurbishing the monument. It was first listed in 1988.

Thomas Unett
Birmingham 1857

Designer: Peter Hollins
Size: Medium
Material: Polished red granite and other stone
Location: St Philip's Cathedral churchyard
Rail: A short walk from all three stations
Bus: Any service to the city centre
Nearest car park: Livery Street

Map contains Ordnance Survey Data © Crown copyright and database 2011, 2012.

The Crimean War began when Britain and France declared war on Russia on the 27th March 1854 to stop the Russian military advance through the Balkans to Turkey. The English fleet was deployed to destroy the Russian Black Sea Fleet in their base at Sebastopol.

On the 21st April 1854 Lieutenant-Colonel Thomas Unett of the 19th Foot embarked on the steamship Victoria off Woolwich, for Constantinople and the Crimea. From that day until he returned to England a year later, he wrote in his journal every day and filled his sketchbook with drawings of tents, dead horses, Turkish and Bulgarian costumes in the local landscape. The journal and sketchbook are in the care of the Staffordshire County Record Office.

Thomas Unett was born in 1800 at No.6 Old Square, Birmingham, a son of John Wilkes Unett, a Lichfield man; a solicitor, a founder member of the Birmingham Law Society and a property developer in Staffordshire and Newtown in Birmingham. His sons did not follow their father in the legal profession but continued the Unett tradition of distinguished military service, Thomas in the Crimea, Walter in India. Thomas' journal is well-written in beautiful handwriting. In June he sent two months of journal home to Mary, his wife in which he describes disembarking at Constantinople with his "valuable grey mare", setting up camp in Scutari and later in Devna, where he hunted wild boar while he waited. By the 25th July there is cholera in the camp, too many dying to press on to Sebastopol. In September they land in the Crimea and fight at the battle of Alma where his mare dies and the men strip the dead Russians of their superior boots, for winter is coming and the Crimean winter is cold and very wet. Throughout the journal he comments on the Turks and their institutions; on the deficiencies in the army supplies; the difficulties getting the wounded to Scutari. In his opinion no commander in the

Thomas Unett's memorial is of polished red granite with a gilded inscription. On the shaft are the names of the Crimean War battles in which he fought: ALMA · INKERMANN · SEBASTOPOL. The obelisk was designed by Peter Hollins (1800-1886), the leading local sculptor of his day. Other memorials in Birmingham, such as that at Witton (page 47) are similar in style and material.

Camp before Sebastopol, 29 December 1854: pages from Lt-Col. Unett's sketchbook.
Reproduced by kind permission of Staffordshire Record Office D3610/16/2

army should be over the age of sixty. In December 1854 there are long descriptions of how they survived the awful conditions by foraging for food, shelter, charcoal and wood.

The journal ends in March 1855 when he left Constantinople and arrived home in April with a letter describing the poor leadership and supplies, and the terrible conditions. He gave it to Richard Cobden, M.P., pacifist and 'Apostle of Free Trade'.

In June, Thomas returned to the Crimea, to the siege of Sebastopol where he died on the 8th September. He was buried in the cemetery at Sebastopol.

On the 5th December 1855, the Morning Post (London), under the heading 'Monument to Colonel Unett' quoted "The Birmingham Gazette announces that the gallant General Windham, the hero of the Redan, has forwarded a contribution to the fund for erecting a monument in honour of the late Colonel Thomas Unett. It will be recollected that on the morning of the attack, Colonel Unett and General (then Colonel) Windham drew lots for the post of honour as leader of the storming party, and the choice fell to Colonel Unett. While Colonel Unett was being carried back wounded, he was met by General Windham, with whom he very warmly shook hands, and but a few minutes later he received his second and mortal wound…"

On Tuesday the 8th January 1856, The Morning Post (London), Military Intelligence recorded a meeting of subscribers to the fund for erecting a monument to Lieutenant-Colonel Thomas Unett held at Dee's hotel. The Rev. E.A. Bagot from the Chair opened the business by remarking that a few days ago he was in conversation with Brigadier-General Shirley who spoke warmly of Colonel Unett with tears in his eyes and ascribed to him every quality that would adorn a soldier and gentleman. His father and brother had agreed to leave the choice of site and monument to the subscribers. £250 had been raised and a corner plot of land within the enclosure of St. Philip's churchyard was chosen for the granite obelisk.

The unveiling of the monument took place in the churchyard on Saturday the 15th August 1857. "Expressions of approval of its appearance are very general".

8 William Cheshire
Stratford-upon-Avon 1858

Size: Small
Material: Warwick Sandstone?
Location: Holy Trinity churchyard, Old Town
Bus: Stagecoach and Johnson's services
Rail: Chiltern Railways and London Midland services to Stratford
Car: Use Park & Ride Easter–September

Map contains Ordnance Survey Data © Crown copyright and database 2011, 2012.

The inscriptions read:

IN MEMORY *of*
Wм. CHESHIRE JUNʀ
who died after a short illness
June 23 1858 *in the*
29th. year of his age

*Although brought up as an operative
printer, he was led by his love for Nature to
the study of Botany, in which science he
attained considerable proficiency, but
unfortunately died too young to leave
any lasting record of his labours.
His memory however lives in the hearts of his
associates and friends, by whom this
Monument was erected.*

*"The summer's flower is
to the summer sweet
Though to itself it only
live and die:"*
Sonnet 94

9 Edward Willes
Leamington 1875

Designer: John Cundall
Size: Medium
Material: Obelisk is a monolith of pale grey granite. Base is of "Derbyshire stone" and other stones
Location: Jephson Gardens, Royal Leamington Spa
Nearest rail station: Leamington Spa
Bus: Stagecoach and West Midlands Travel
Coach trips also visit Leamington
Nearest car parks: St Peter's and Rosefield Street

Map contains Ordnance Survey Data © Crown copyright and database 2011, 2012.

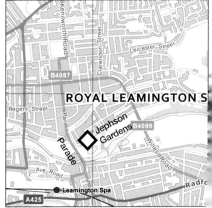

The *Leamington Spa Courier* considered that Edward Willes was Leamington's greatest benefactor. After 1820, when he inherited Newbold Comyn, he engaged architects to lay out his land for elegant houses and open spaces that would extend the speculative development of the New Town following the opening of the New Pump Rooms and Baths in 1814.

The Willes family left the town in 1827 (a mistake, according to Edward's son William) leaving agents to implement the plan. Edward effectively gave Holly Walk and Euston Place to the town, as well as the sites of churches and the garden of the Regent Hotel. He placed covenants on his land by the river to preserve its open outlook, including the Newbold Gardens, former meadows which had been laid out in simple style around 1832 as walks for subscribers. In 1846 Edward, very ill, agreed to the neglected Gardens being acquired by trustees and remodelled as a testimonial to Dr Henry Jephson, whose promotion of the spa waters had brought prosperity to the town. Renamed the Jephson Gardens, they opened in 1847, just months after Edward died. From time to time the *Courier* reminded its readers that Leamington lacked any memorial that acknowledged his munificence.

William Willes planned to return to Leamington following his mother's death in 1873. He made it known that he hoped that the town would erect a memorial to his father. The Trustees of the Gardens obliged with an obelisk but refused to agree to any inscription which corrected the impression that had gained currency that the Gardens were the gift of Dr Jephson, who despite old age remained chairman. When the obelisk was unveiled in June 1875 the *Courier* pointed out that the plaque did not state why the obelisk had been erected.

The town belatedly acknowledged "Leamington's greatest benefactor" with this fine obelisk – "a Victorian beauty" in the opinion of Richard Barnes.

The original 1875 inscription reads:

ERECTED IN HONOUR OF
EDWARD WILLES ESQUIRE
OF NEWBOLD COMYN

The second inscription was added in 1879 and explains:

TO WHOM LEAMINGTON IS INDEBTED
FOR THE SITE OF THESE GARDENS

Meanwhile, William and the local Board were co-operating on improvements to Willes Road and Willes Bridge. A plaque which fully acknowledged Edward's generosity was placed on the bridge. Courteous and grateful, William remained dissatisfied about the Gardens because he had a faulty understanding of their history. The trustees published their account: William refuted it point by point and threatened them with a new lease. After Dr Jephson died in 1878 the Trustees offered no opposition to a second inscription. Honour satisfied, William's ire abated. With his wife and baby son he at last moved back to Newbold Comyn House as another obelisk – that to Henry Bright – became the focus of his wrath (page 43).

The Philips family
Welcombe Bank 1876

Size: Large
Material: Warwick Sandstone?
Cornice and plinth are of a harder stone
Location: Welcombe Hills Country Park
Rail: Chiltern and London Midland services
to Stratford
Bus: Johnsons and Stagecoach services
to Stratford
Car: Park & Ride into Stratford, April-September
Parking: Maidenhead Road & Ingon Lane (limited)

Map contains Ordnance Survey Data © Crown copyright and database 2011, 2012.

The Welcombe Bank obelisk is a memorial erected by Robert Needham Philips in 1876 to commemorate his brother Mark and his father Robert. Said to be of Welsh granite though clearly two kinds of sandstone, 120 feet (37 metres) high, it is an outstanding feature in the landscape overlooking the Avon valley. Three sides of the pedestal have plaques inscribed with details of the men's lives and achievements; the fourth side has the family coat of arms.

The elder Robert Philips was a wealthy cotton manufacturer from Lancashire "seeking a dignified house in the desirable Midlands". He bought the manor of Snitterfield from George, Earl of Coventry for £65,000 in 1816. He demolished the Stuart manor and used the materials to extend Park House. On his death in 1844 his son Mark inherited the house and Snitterfield village.

Mark was born in 1800 at The Park, Prestwich between Manchester and Bury and was the first M.P. to be elected to represent Manchester after the Reform Act of 1832. For fifteen years he sat as a liberal interested in education, civil and religious liberty and an opponent of "taxes upon knowledge". He was a pioneer 'left-winger' upholding working class rights. He sympathised with the French Revolution after visiting Paris in 1830. According to the plaque he had "a rare flow of wit and humour".

In 1845 Mark bought the Welcombe estate from Charles Thomas Warde who had inherited Clopton House. A drawing of 1821 of the original house portrays a picturesque scene with a lake in the foreground and the gothic house partly hidden by shrubs and surrounded by trees.

The 120-foot obelisk on the Welcombe Bank commands a view of south Warwickshire.

The Philips family crest with the "untranslateable" motto
SIMPLEX MUNDITIIS.
PHOTOS: Jean Nicholson

Mark retired from politics in 1847, demolished the Welcombe house and continued to live in Snitterfield. It was not until 1866 that he employed Henry Clutton, a local architect to draw up plans for a country seat. After Clutton withdrew, the house was completed by a Manchester architect, Thomas Newby in 1869 at a cost of £100,000. W.A.Nesfield, a popular and successful designer, was employed to design a garden for the new house. Nesfield surrounded the pleasure garden with more shrubberies and trees, a picturesque element.

Mark did not enjoy it for long. He died on the 23rd December 1873 leaving the estate to his brother Robert Needham Philips, cotton manufacturer and M.P. for Bury. In 1876 Robert erected the obelisk, now a Grade II memorial at a cost of £7,000. He died in 1890; his eulogy was added to the southeast side.

Henry Buck

Birmingham 1876

Size: Small
Material: Limestone? on a pedestal of polished red granite and other stone
Location: St Philip's Cathedral churchyard
Rail: A short walk from all three stations
Bus: Any service to the city centre
Nearest car park: Livery Street

Map contains Ordnance Survey Data © Crown copyright and database 2011, 2012.

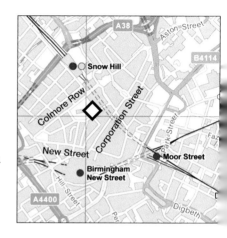

The inscription reads:

ERECTED BY THE MEMBERS
OF THE BIRMINGHAM
DISTRICT OF THE
MANCHESTER ORDER OF
ODD FELLOWS TO THE
MEMORY OF PAST GRAND
MASTER HENRY BUCK FOR
25 YEARS THEIR FAITHFUL
AND ESTEEMED SECRETARY
DIED JANUARY 22ND 1876
AGED 65 YEARS

One of the four obelisks in St Philip's Cathedral churchyard is a public memorial to Mr Henry Buck, secretary to the Birmingham District of the Manchester Order of Odd Fellows. The Manchester Unity Order of Odd Fellows was one of the first and oldest Friendly Societies. Through the modest contributions of their members they could extend help to those who were ill, injured, bereaved or unemployed. The Friendly Societies overcame suppression and discrimination to become the forerunners of trades unions, insurance companies, provident organisations and mutual savings societies. When the first Labour government was setting up the National Health Service in 1948, it was the actuarial tables of the Oddfellows that were consulted to determine the level of National Insurance contributions. The term Odd Fellows comes from the fact that in smaller towns and villages there were too few Fellows in the same trade to form a local Guild. Instead they formed a local Guild from an assortment of different trades: the Odd Fellows. Henry Buck was a popular secretary and director; he was a bold and powerful advocate of financial reform who could give a robust defence to any criticism of the Order.

Henry Bright
Royal Leamington Spa 1880

Designer: John Cundall
Size: Medium
Material: Pink granite on a sandstone pedestal
Location: Facing Parade between Regent Grove and Hamilton Terrace
Nearest rail station: Leamington Spa
Bus: Stagecoach & West Midlands Travel
Coach trips also visit Leamington
Nearest car parks: St Peter's & Rosefield Street

Map contains Ordnance Survey Data © Crown copyright and database 2011, 2012.

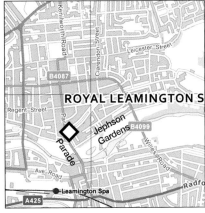

Leamington has four obelisks. Two of them are war memorials, at Whitnash and St Mary's Church. The other two are a short distance apart and were built within five years of each other. Is there a connection between them?

The story of the Willes obelisk, unveiled in 1875, is told on page 38. The obelisk erected as a testimonial to Henry Bright caused controversy at its inception, during its construction, and after its completion in December 1880. William Willes tried and failed to stop it being built.

Henry Bright's long residence in Leamington began in 1831 when his father Isaac Bright, a goldsmith in Sheffield since 1786, started up in business at 2 Union Parade as watchmaker, jeweller and silversmith. After Isaac retired due to blindness the business operated under the names of Henry and his younger brother Edward. Isaac, who had been a member of the earliest community of Jews in Sheffield, died aged 86 in 1849 (the year of the cholera epidemic in Leamington).

By 1855 Edward had set up on his own in Brighton: Henry was a family man and well-established in business. He ventured into politics, being elected to the local Board of Health with the support of a ratepayers' association. He quickly began a long career as a campaigner for improvements to the lives and health of ordinary people; perhaps he was moved by deaths in his family. At various times subsequently he was a member of the Burial Board, the Hospital Board, the School Board and chairman of the Provident Dispensary for the Poor. He was familiar with the work and writings of Edwin Chadwick on public health and social reform. He campaigned against the pollution of the River

ABOVE: *Portrait photograph of Mr Henry Bright.*
© Leamington Spa Art Gallery & Museum (Warwick District Council)

RIGHT: *Henry Bright and his obelisk at the end of Holly Walk 1881.*
© Leamington Spa Art Gallery & Museum (Warwick District Council)

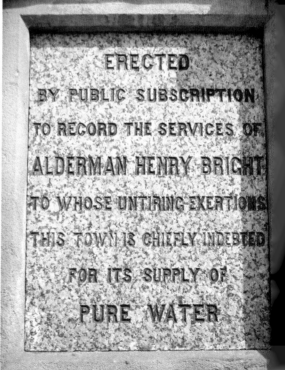

Leam, from which much of Leamington was privately supplied with water. He overcame strong opposition to establish a borehole which secured an abundant supply of pure, if hard, water. It was turned on for public use in November 1878. In March 1879, on behalf of a grateful populace, Henry's friends resolved to give public recognition to his efforts in the form of an ornamental fountain in his honour; subscriptions were invited. A few days later the waterworks was officially opened amid much celebration.

In 1879 the obelisk in honour of Edward Willes was in the news when the Trustees of the Jephson Gardens added a second inscription acknowledging Edward's munificence. Coincidentally, in May 1879 the Leamington *Courier* published a report of the restoration of Cleopatra's Needle. By January 1880 the proposed memorial to Mr Bright had become an obelisk and drinking fountain. William Willes wrote to the Town Council objecting to an obelisk at the proposed site, the entrance to Holly Walk, which was much narrower than it is now. The response was to amend the design to make the base and pedestal more slender and to widen the entrance to the walk.

A General Election was expected in 1880. At that time the South Warwickshire constituency included Leamington and returned two MPs. The incumbents were Tories. William Willes, since his return to Leamington in 1875, had become President of the South Warwickshire Conservative Association. Henry Bright was a Radical and a Liberal. Following direct canvassing by Henry the Liberals put up a candidate, the Hon. Gilbert Leigh. On polling day, 10 April, rival supporters clashed in the streets; the mayor had to read the Riot Act from the (old) Town Hall steps. Leigh was elected along with one of the Tory candidates; Liberals in Leamington were jubilant.

When preparations for constructing the obelisk got under way in May 1880 there was a sense that it would be a monument to Liberal triumph both locally and nationally. Early morning felling of trees aroused concern. Construction having begun, the contractor John Fell (also a Liberal town councillor) was served with notice of trespass by Mr Brown, William Willes's solicitor. Then William applied for an injunction restraining its erection without his permission. He argued that the Corporation's rights to Holly Walk extended only to the surface of the ground. The subsoil was his: therefore in digging for the foundations the contractor was trespassing. In September, the judges took a more commonsense view and dismissed the application with costs: a humiliating outcome for William. The obelisk was completed in December and was much admired.

From New Street to Witton
1882

Size: Medium
Location: Witton Cemetery is 3 miles (5km) north of Birmingham city centre
Access: Open daily 10-4 or longer
Gates on Moor Lane B6 and The Ridgeway B23
Nearest rail station: Witton (New St-Walsall line)
Bus: Service 7 from city centre or 11, outer circle route
Parking: In the cemetery, anywhere on the main avenue

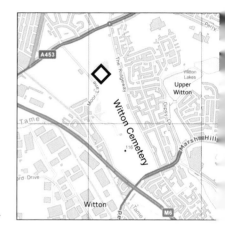

Map contains Ordnance Survey Data © Crown copyright and database 2011, 2012.

The station we know as Birmingham New Street opened fully in 1854. It was a successful central station and the London & North Western Railway Company sought to extend it. In 1881 they bought the adjoining Old Meeting House chapel, schoolhouse and burial ground. For the congregation the outcome was intensely regretted.

> *Not only are all the historical associations in connection with the place about to be swept away, but the removal of the dead is a painful matter… The chapel about to be taken down is… a protest in this town on behalf of liberty of conscience… Its pulpit has been filled by a succession of enlightened men, who have sought the simple truths of religion without creeds, and have rendered a valuable service in sustaining the intellectual life of Birmingham. Our chapel has been a power in the town…*

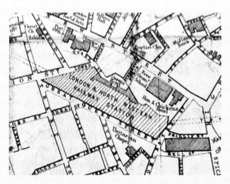

A map of 1863 shows the Chapel south of New Street station. WCRO CR1086/11.

The school and burial ground of the Old Meeting House. / archive.org

The mortal remains from the Old Meeting House burial ground were reinterred at Witton in 1882. They are arranged in an enclosure defined by obeliskal bollards. The inscriptions on a granite obelisk tell the story:

OLD MEETING HOUSE BIRMINGHAM

THE LONDON AND NORTH WESTERN RAILWAY COMPANY HAVING ACQUIRED THE OLD MEETING HOUSE SCHOOL BUILDINGS AND GRAVE-YARD UNDER AUTHORITY OF PARLIAMENT FOR THE PURPOSE OF ENLARGING NEW STREET RAILWAY STATION THE REMAINS OF THE DEAD WITH THE TOMBSTONES AND MONUMENTS WERE IN THE YEAR 1882 REMOVED UNDER SUPERINTENDENCE OF THE TRUSTEES TO THIS ENCLOSURE WITH THE APPROVAL OF THE TOWN COUNCIL OF THE BOROUGH OF BIRMINGHAM

OLD MEETING HOUSE BIRMINGHAM

— THIS MEMORIAL —
IS ERECTED TO POINT OUT THE SPOT IN WHICH ARE DEPOSITED THE MORTAL REMAINS OF THOSE PERSONS WHO WERE BURIED IN THE GRAVE-YARD ADJOINING THE OLD MEETING HOUSE BIRMINGHAM. THE RE-INTERMENTS WERE MADE IN VAULTS AND GRAVES CORRESPONDING AS NEARLY AS POSSIBLE WITH THOSE IN THE FORMER GRAVE-YARD. THE EXISTING RIGHTS OF INTERMENT ARE RESERVED TO THIS ENCLOSURE BY ARRANGEMENT WITH THE TRUSTEES
1882.

14 Burnaby of the Blues
Birmingham 1885

Designer: J.A. Chatwin
Size: Large
Material: Portland Stone & Hopton Wood Stone
Location: St Philip's Cathedral churchyard
Rail: A short walk from all three stations
Bus: Any service to the city centre
Nearest car park: Livery Street

Map contains Ordnance Survey Data © Crown copyright and database 2011, 2012.

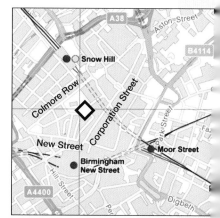

Portrait of Frederick Burnaby by James Jacques Tissot, 1870.
© National Portrait Gallery, London

Colonel Frederick Gustavus Burnaby was a Victorian celebrity, a soldier renowned for his strength and heroic figure: at 6 feet 4 inches with a 46-inch chest, he was "the bravest man in England".

He was born in 1842 into a wealthy family, the son of a fox-hunting parson in Bedford. He was well-educated and a proficient linguist, speaking the main European languages as well as Russian, some Turkish and Arabic. At the age of 16 he passed his army exam and purchased a cornetcy in the Royal Horse Guards (The Blues) and rose to captain by 1866. During the long leaves of the Household Cavalry over the winter months, he travelled and enjoyed a bohemian lifestyle; he was a journalist and a balloonist. His first ascent was in 1864. In 1882 he crossed the Channel and published an account of his adventurous flight.

In 1868 with journalist friend Thomas Gibson Bowles he founded the weekly satirical magazine *Vanity Fair*. Bowles met James Tissot in France, invited him to England and commissioned full-page coloured caricatures for the magazine and a portrait of Burnaby. It presents him reclining on a white sofa in his Blues uniform, languidly smoking a cigarette below a map of the world.

As a journalist Burnaby travelled to Spain as an accredited *Times* correspondent reporting on the civil war in 1874 and early in 1875 to Khartoum and Sobat where he met General Gordon. Later that year he travelled to Russia to investigate rumours of Russia's expansion southwards, a threat to the British in India on the Northwest frontier. He recounted his expedition in his lively best-selling book *A Ride to Khiva*. It was a sensation and made him a celebrity commemorated in verse, song and Staffordshire pottery. A hero to the public, he dined with Queen Victoria. Another

Relief portrait of Burnaby on the pedestal of his obelisk.

expedition and book, *On Horseback through Asia Minor* 1876-7 was followed by a journey to Bulgaria on behalf of the Red Cross during the Russo-Turkish War 1877.

Burnaby's connection with Birmingham was political. He believed in Tory democracy; he admired Disraeli's foreign policy and detested Gladstone. He decided to stand for parliament and chose to contest the radical stronghold of Birmingham against John Bright and Chamberlain in 1880. He lost but gained 15,735 votes. In 1883 he helped to found the Primrose League, whose aim was to obtain the support of the people for Conservative principles: the primrose had been Disraeli's favourite flower. At a meeting in Birmingham in the same year Burnaby was elected to the Council of the National Union of Conservative Associations.

In 1884 with General Gordon in danger in the Sudan he travelled to Egypt on his own account, undeterred by the refusal of the authorities to send him on active service, and joined the second expedition up the Nile. He was killed by a Mahdi spear at Abu Klea on the 18th January 1885. The poet William McGonagall paid tribute in *The Battle of Abu Klea*:

> *Oh! it was an exciting and terrible sight,*
> *To see Colonel Burnaby engaged in the fight:*
> *With sword in hand, fighting with might and main,*
> *Until killed by a spear-thrust in the jugular vein.*
> *A braver soldier ne'er fought on a battle-field,*
> *Death or glory was his motto, rather than yield;*
> *A man of noble stature and manly to behold.*
> *And an honour to his country be it told.*

Burnaby was not commemorated in London because, it is thought, his political remarks had offended the Prince of Wales and his circle. To commemorate him in Birmingham a public subscription — "no more than a guinea, no less than a penny" — raised £501 from 2,500 subscribers in less than a month. A committee was formed who chose a design offered free of charge by local architect J.A. Chatwin. The obelisk was built of Portland and Hopton Wood stone by R.A. Bridgeman of Lichfield who added the upper moulding of carved primroses to the pedestal.

The unveiling ceremony was performed by Colonel Burnaby's friend and comrade Captain Charles Beresford, R.N. on Wednesday 11th November 1885. The memorial was handed over to the care of St Philip's Church.

The Twentieth Century

War Memorials

Many First World War memorials are obelisks. Nationally, war memorials had already been erected to honour the six thousand men who died in the Boer War, 1899-1902. It was the first time since the Crimean War that the deaths of soldiers had been recognised by British society. Some of the memorials were obelisks that continued the Victorian association of worth and sacrifice. During the First World War, 1914-18, the authorities decided that the bodies of those who were killed would not be repatriated. It recognised the reality of shattered remains and that the bodies of many combatants would never be found. Local communities could commemorate their losses in their own way. At the end of the war a number of committees and commissions addressed the principles, design and implementation of memorials to the millions who died around the world. In Britain the Victoria and Albert Museum and the Royal Academy held exhibitions of memorial designs in 1919 and 1920; sculpture featured strongly.

Committees in villages, towns and cities raised funds for local memorials and decided what form they should take: there was no direction by the authorities. Some were 'utilitarian', such as hospitals, parks and village halls; the majority were architectural, ranging from chapels and temples through an extraordinary variety of monumental forms to simple crosses and obelisks. Sir Edwin Lutyens, one of the architects appointed to the Imperial (later Commonwealth) War Graves Commission, particularly favoured the obelisk as being monumental without being associated with a particular religion or denomination. The perception of obelisks had changed in the centuries since the Renaissance. Amongst other memorials, Lutyens designed the Cenotaph in London's Whitehall and the war memorial in Northampton. An obelisk was relatively inexpensive and simple for a mason to construct; sometimes it was chosen to avoid differences of religious opinion on committees. Richard Barnes comments: "Ecclesiastical authorities often chose the obelisk to placemark, as a cross might imply a burial." There are notable obelisk war memorials in Blackpool, Manchester, Scarborough, Mousehole in Cornwall and Euston Station in London.

As well as the obelisk war memorials whose stories are told individually here, others may be found at Ansty (unveiled in 2012), Baddesley Ensor; Pype Hayes, Birmingham; Church Lawford; the 'Triumph and Gloria' memorial in London Road Cemetery, Coventry; Exhall, Coventry; Hurley; Kenilworth; St Mary's Church, Leamington; Napton; Nuneaton Colliery, Whittleford Road, Nuneaton; Pooley Hall Colliery, Polesworth; Priors Hardwick; Rowington; Sutton-under-Brailes; Whitnash and Wormleighton – and there may be others. Village war memorials may list several men from the same family. With Warwickshire seen as the centre of England, two memorials have a national dimension: that to the 29th Division near Stretton-on-Dunsmore and the Cyclists' memorial at Meriden.

Some War Memorials

1. *Priors Hardwick, by the village street.*
2. *Hurley, in a cemetery.*
3. *Sutton under Brailes, on a village green.*
   PHOTO: David Stowell / geograph.org.uk
4. *Kenilworth, in a park by a main road.*
   PHOTO: John Brightley / geograph.org.uk
5. *Exhall near Bedworth, on a traffic island.*
6. *Rowington, in a churchyard.*
7. *Baddesley Ensor, in a churchyard.*
   PHOTO: Jean Nicholson

8. *Private memorial to an officer killed in France, 1918, Beaudesert churchyard.*
   PHOTO: Douglas Bridgewater

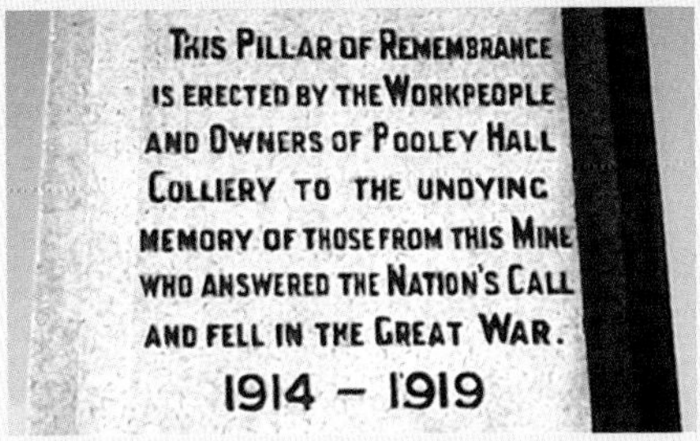

THIS PILLAR OF REMEMBRANCE
IS ERECTED BY THE WORKPEOPLE
AND OWNERS OF POOLEY HALL
COLLIERY TO THE UNDYING
MEMORY OF THOSE FROM THIS MINE
WHO ANSWERED THE NATION'S CALL
AND FELL IN THE GREAT WAR.
1914 — 1919

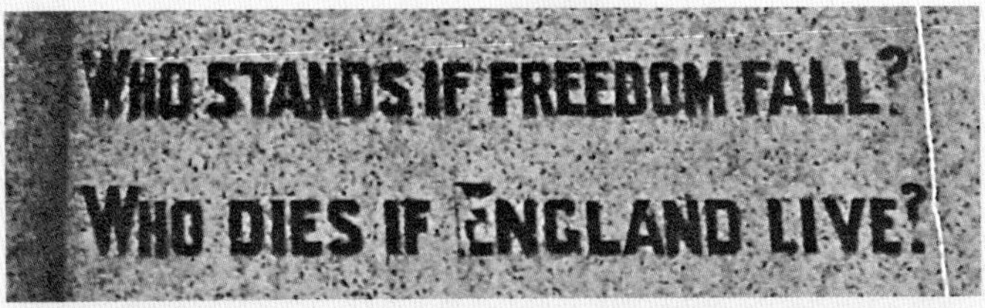

WHO STANDS IF FREEDOM FALL?

WHO DIES IF ENGLAND LIVE?

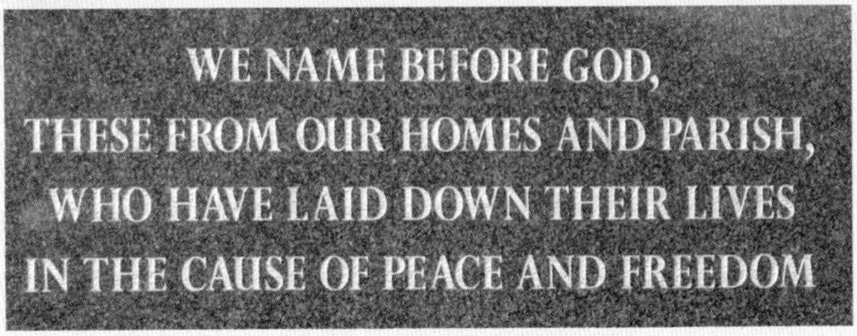

WE NAME BEFORE GOD,
THESE FROM OUR HOMES AND PARISH,
WHO HAVE LAID DOWN THEIR LIVES
IN THE CAUSE OF PEACE AND FREEDOM

Inscriptions on war memorials

RIGHT: *One of the four bronze panels originally on the memorial at Radford, Coventry.*
TOP: *Letters inscribed in grey granite and painted, near Pooley Hall.*
PHOTOS: Peter Warrilow
ABOVE: *Gilded inscription, Pype Hayes, 2000.*
BELOW: *Metal letters inserted into a granite tablet, Church Lawford.*

IN
EVER
GRATEFUL MEMORY
OF OUR MEN FROM
CHURCH LAWFORD
AND
KINGS NEWNHAM
WHO FELL IN
THE GREAT WAR 1914-1918.

T.C. GANDY
E GLOVER.
S. GLOVER. = E
GODDEN. = E.
GODDEN. = G.
GODDEN. = H.
GODDEN. = E.J.
GODFREY. = J.
GOUGH = A.G.
RAINGER. = C.H.
GRAINGER. = J.
GRAINGER. = T
GRAINGER. = W
GRINDLEY. = W.
HALL. = W.J. HAL-
LIDAY. = E HARRIS.
H. HARRIS. = D.J.
HAYDEN = L.J.H-
AYDEN. = R. HIGG-
INS. = D.C. HILL = A.
HOBBS. = A.H. HOL-
MES. = W. HOUGHT-
ON. = J.H. HUGHES.
T. HUGHES. = W. HU-
GHES. = J.E. IDIENS.
G. INNOCENT. = A.I-
RELAND. = W. JAKEM-
AN. = F.H. JONES. = H.J.
JONES. = †H. JONES.
A. KENNY. = †E. KILLP-
ACK. = G. KILLPACK. =

Radford War Memorial
Coventry 1919

Size: Small
Material: Pink-brown Runcorn Sandstone
Location: Open space by Sherwood Jones Close
CV6, off Engleton Road
Nearest rail station: Coventry
Bus: Stagecoach Stratford-Coventry service 16
or National Express Coventry-Keresley
service 16A
Parking: Nearby church or supermarket

Map contains Ordnance Survey Data © Crown copyright and database 2011, 2012.

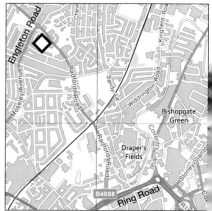

The Radford war memorial is neighbour to the great brick barn and bell-tower of St Nicholas' Church, consecrated in 1954. The memorial is a simple stone obelisk on a square base of three steps. Each of the four faces of the obelisk originally bore a cast bronze panel giving the names of the 152 men of Radford who fought in the Great War of 1914-1918, with a cross prefixed to the names of the 17 men who gave their lives.

The memorial was the brainchild of the Radford War Memorial Committee, and was the gift of Councillor C. Vernon Pugh, who supervised the unveiling on the 19th of December, 1919 on its original site, the southeast corner of Radford Common across Engleton Road from its present position. It was designed and constructed in pink-brown Runcorn stone under the direction of Mr T. R. J. Meakin, architect, of Coventry. The stonework was by Messrs White and Sons, Yardley; the bronze panels were executed by Messrs Baker and Sons, St Paul's Square, Birmingham; and the foundation work was by Messrs Garlick of Coventry.

At the unveiling the Bishop of Coventry and His Worship the Mayor made short speeches. The Radford memorial was the first in Coventry to be publicly handed over to the city. The Mayor, in his remarks, observed that "there were numerous Cenotaphs about the city, but they were only of a temporary nature"; the Radford memorial was a substantial and perfect gift. Floral tributes were laid by the many people attending, who sang hymns and the National Anthem accompanied by the Salvation Army band.

Other villages in Coventry's orbit had their own memorials but they were partially eclipsed by the opening of the War Memorial Park, Stivichall, in 1921, with its towering Cenotaph,

ABOVE: *The unveiling in 1919: Councillor Vernon Pugh presents the obelisk to the Mayor, witnessed by the Bishop of Coventry and others.*
Coventry History Centre: Coventry Graphic

LEFT: *The memorial in 2005.*

unveiled by Earl Haig in 1927. This became the main focus for the city's Remembrance Day ceremonies. After the Second World War there seems to have been a resurgence of Remembrance Sunday services at the suburban and village memorials. In 1945 the *Coventry Standard*, 17th November, reported the first service for many years at the Radford war memorial, organised by the No.9 branch of the British Legion; the service was conducted by the Rev. J. J. Hunt, vicar of the Victorian church of St Nicholas that had been destroyed in the blitz of 14th November, 1940. The blitz was remembered for some years in an open-air service in the ruins of the cathedral. Because of the coincidence of dates it was often reported by the newspapers in the same week as Remembrance Day events. In an editorial on the subject in 1952, 14th November, the *Coventry Standard* regretted that: "…some of the uniformity which marked these occasions before the war has been lost. London has its major service at the Cenotaph; other towns and cities hold some joint service. In Coventry in recent years there has been a tendency for individual organisations to please themselves…"

Services have continued at Radford. In 1981, the *Coventry Evening Telegraph*, 9th April, reported that the Radford branch of the British Legion had asked the City Council if the memorial might be moved into the grounds of St Nicholas' Church. They felt that it would be less exposed to vandalism there, and it would be a more suitable site; the previous November, after heavy rain, wreath-layers at the Remembrance Day service had been "ankle-deep in mud". The City Council acceded to the request. Sadly, since the first visit for this book, one bronze panel has been stolen; the other three have been removed for safe keeping.

16 The Cyclists' War Memorial
Meriden 1921

Size: Medium
Material: Rough grey granite
Location: The Green, Meriden village
Nearest rail station: Hampton in Arden
Bus: National Express service 900,
Coventry-Birmingham
Parking: Car park in the Recreation Ground off
the roundabout, west end of village

Map contains Ordnance Survey Data © Crown copyright and database 2011, 2012.

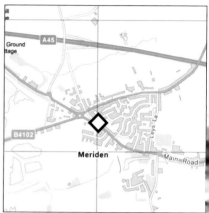

Self-propelled wheeled machines evolved through the 19th century as playthings of the wealthy. The affordable Rover Safety Bicycle, produced by Starley and Sutton of Coventry in 1885, launched an industry and an era. Working and middle class people, now with more leisure, took up cycling. Clubs were formed; whole families cycled. Like Tanworth-in-Arden, Meriden was a popular rendezvous for Birmingham and Coventry cyclists, offering accommodation, refreshments – and repairs.

The Scouts adopted bicycles for patrols and expeditions, as did some Territorial Army formations to increase mobility at low cost. At the outbreak of the Great War in 1914 they took their bikes with them to the front. The Army Cycle Corps employed cyclists as scouts and messengers. There were both regular and Territorial cycling battalions, regiments and smaller units, classed as either cavalry or infantry.

After 1918 communities everywhere considered how to commemorate their dead. The Cyclists' Touring Club raised £1,200 by subscription for a unique memorial to cyclists: a 30-foot high obelisk of concrete faced with Cornish granite. Meriden, at the centre of England, was the natural location. Lord Aylesford gave the site.

It was unveiled by Lord Birkenhead, the Lord Chancellor and president of the memorial fund, before "a vast multitude" who had ridden or walked to Meriden on that hot, sunny Saturday, May 21st, 1921. He recalled the service which cyclists undertook. "In every scene of the theatre of war, in France, in Flanders, in the south and in the east, in the days before the means of mechanical transport was brought to its later perfection, they carried in the presence of death itself those vital messages, the secrecy of which alone meant so much to their comrades…" He remembered the degree of dependence placed on the humble bicyclist in France in 1914 and 1915. "Theirs was a lonely life; theirs very often was a lonely death…the men in the trenches had the support of others, side by side, sharing the same horrors. The cyclists' work with all its dangers was performed in solitude…Remember these men…" The service concluded with clubs placing wreaths and flowers on the memorial. Newspaper reports remarked on the thousands of bare bronzed heads and the age and fitness of some of those attending.

A service has been held every year since on the Saturday nearest to Empire Day, May 24th. In recent years the weekend has been presented more as a celebration of cycling.

LEFT: *The sombre memorial of rough grey granite on the Green at Meriden.*

ABOVE: *Thousands of people attended the unveiling on the Green, 21st May 1921.*
Solihull Heritage & Local Studies

IN REMEMBRANCE
OF THOSE
CYCLISTS
WHO GAVE THEIR LIVES
IN WORLD WAR II
1939 - 1945

ABOVE: *Many First World War memorials have an added inscription or plaque to commemorate the fallen of the Second World War.*

The 29th Division
Stretton-on-Dunsmore 1921

Size: Medium
Material: Portland Stone
Access: Traffic island at the fast, busy junction of A45 and B4455 Fosse Way
Nearest rail station: Coventry
Bus: Mike de Courcey service 580 between Coventry & Rugby
Parking: Off-road by Fosse Way north of the junction, at your own risk

Map contains Ordnance Survey Data © Crown copyright and database 2011, 2012.

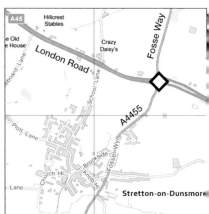

On Empire Day, 24th May 1921, three days after the Cyclists' Memorial was unveiled at Meriden, a rather different ceremony took place beside the London Road (the modern A45) near Stretton-on-Dunsmore. Both sites, in the traditional centre of England, were chosen as being representative of the whole country as well as for their particular associations.

When the First World War broke out in 1914 half of Britain's regular army was garrisoning the Empire. The generals believed that more of these regular troops should be sent to the Western Front to break the stalemate with Germany. As the overseas forces hastened home, Winston Churchill, First Lord of the Admiralty under Asquith, resolved to help Britain's ally Russia. Its navy and its foreign trade needed to pass through the Dardanelles strait between the Black Sea and the Mediterranean but there was a perceived threat from German-trained Turkish forces on the Gallipoli peninsula to the north. A British naval expedition would force a passage through the Dardanelles from the Mediterranean and bombard Constantinople, modern Istanbul, to knock Turkey out of the war.

Disparate elements of the British army assembled as the new 29th Division in Warwickshire and north Oxfordshire while Churchill and the generals argued about where to deploy them, Gallipoli or France. Seasoned soldiers, some still in tropical kit, were billeted with families in Warwickshire towns and Banbury. Warm hospitality was extended; local economies thrived. In the first months of 1915 the soldiers trained for France in the Warwickshire countryside.

On 12th March King George V reviewed the troops. They stretched four deep for two miles along the London Road from the junction with the Fosse Way. Thereafter the 19,000 men of the 29th Division sailed for the Mediterranean to join troops from

A postcard of the 1920s shows the memorial on a mound by the London Road, flanked by a pair of captured German guns. WCRO PH 352/173/46

The memorial today, in a similar view from the west.

Australia and New Zealand to form the Mediterranean Expeditionary Force. After much delay the MEF was sent to the Dardanelles to support the navy, whose initial attempt on Constantinople had been unexpectedly halted by German and Turkish resistance.

The terrible slaughter of Gallipoli began with the first landings in April 1915. Losses among the ANZAC troops are commemorated every year on 25th April. Thereafter a chaotic, improvised occupation clung to the stony terrain through the heat, dust and flies of summer. Vermin and dysentery were rife. The Allied forces' trenches and shelters were often only yards away from the positions of the fanatical Turkish troops. The loss of life was enormous – over 250,000 on both sides. The recognition of stalemate was as close as the politicians could come to admitting that the Gallipoli campaign was a failure. An evacuation was successfully accomplished at the year's end with great stealth and no loss of human life.

The obelisk commemorates the review by the King, not the tragic failure of an imaginative but mismanaged campaign. At the time people saw it as a memorial to those who fell: a feeling reinforced by the poignant replanting of the avenue across Dunsmore Heath. Many of the elms and pines planted in 1740 had been blown down by a storm in 1912 and were replaced with limes in 1918; some still stand.

The memorial was originally on a mound flanked by captured German guns. The remodelling of the junction in 1984 to reduce accidents left it on the western side of a roundabout. The mound is less prominent because of adjustments to ground levels but the memorial gains in presence. The guns may have been removed during World War II or when the A45 was made a dual-carriageway.

There is an information board by the A45 at the northwest corner of the junction.

A war memorial in all but name.

250,000 Allied soldiers fell at Gallipoli: "incomparable services". At least as many Turkish troops died.

18 Shuckburgh War Memorial
Lower Shuckburgh 1921

Size: Medium

Material: Hornton Stone

Location: At the turning for the church by the lane to Sawbridge and Grandborough off the A425 at Lower Shuckburgh

Bus: Flexibus service 214 Rugby-Priors Hardwick

Nearest rail stations: Rugby, Banbury

Parking: Near the church, considerately

Map contains Ordnance Survey Data © Crown copyright and database 2011, 2012.

The war memorial at the church gate, Lower Shuckburgh, was unveiled by Lt-Gen Sir John Keir KCB on Saturday 19th November, 1921. The *Rugby Advertiser* reported the "very impressive service" in its edition of Friday 25th November, 1921, page 2.

There was rain in the morning but towards 3pm it ceased. The sun appeared as the church bells pealed to announce the coming service of dedication. The church was crowded, many former parishioners from neighbouring villages attending. The Reverend H. J. Watters officiated. The service started at 3pm with the hymn *O God our help in ages past.* Prayers, psalms and versicles followed. The lesson was read by Sir Gerald Shuckburgh, Bart.

The congregation then proceeded outside to the memorial in the following order: the churchwardens, the choir (boys and men), Mr Sykes with the Flecknoe church choir, the vicar, Sir John Keir and Sir Gerald Shuckburgh, ex-servicemen, schoolchildren and the general congregation, meanwhile singing the hymn *Through the night.*

At the memorial Sir John Keir gave a touching address. It was a great honour to be invited to unveil it, he said; local men had given their lives, and he felt deep sympathy for their families and friends, but he considered that they might remember with pride, not sorrow, their boys' great sacrifice. After the address the unveiling took place followed by the *Last Post,* sounded by two buglers. Finally, wreaths and crosses were laid.

The memorial is an obelisk in Hornton stone standing on three bases. Altogether it is 15 feet high and decorated on the face, towards the top, with a small bronze wreath of laurels. An inscription records the names of the fallen.

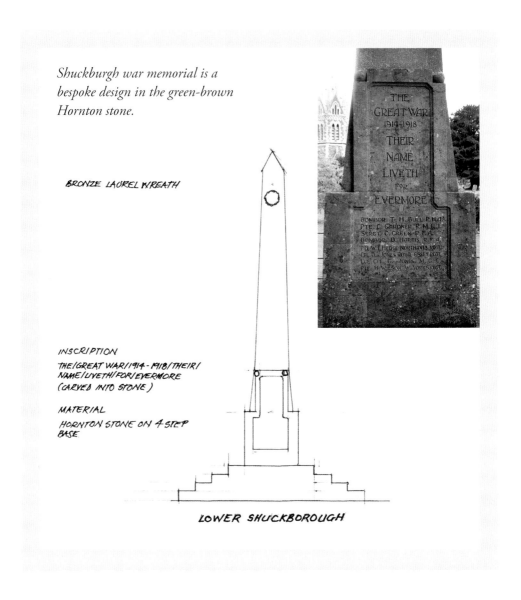

Shuckburgh war memorial is a bespoke design in the green-brown Hornton stone.

BRONZE LAUREL WREATH

INSCRIPTION
THE/GREAT WAR/1914 - 1918/THEIR/
NAME/LIVETH/FOR/EVERMORE
(CARVED INTO STONE)

MATERIAL
HORNTON STONE ON 4 STEP
BASE

THE
GREAT WAR
1914-1918
THEIR
NAME
LIVETH
FOR
EVERMORE

BOMBDR. T. H. BULL R.H.A.
PTE. C. GARDNER R.M.L.I.
SERGT. C. GREEN R.F.A.
BOMBDR. D. HORRIS R.F.A.
PTE. W. HEDGE NORTHANTS REGT.
CPL. D. JONES ROYAL ESSEX REGT.
LCE. CPL. C. JONES. M.G.C.
PTE. H. WILSON W. YORKS REGT.

LOWER SHUCKBOROUGH

Since 1921

In Coventry two almost identical obelisks were erected in 1932-3. The Second World War broke out at the end of the decade; after 1945 many names were added to First World War memorials. There is a new and general war memorial at Pype Hayes north-east of Birmingham. Not far out of the county an obelisk of classical form has been in the public eye since 2007 at the Armed Forces Memorial in the National Memorial Arboretum at Alrewas, Staffordshire. Other 20th century memorials include a confident creation to mark the new millennium at Ratley on the Oxfordshire border; the war memorial unveiled at Ansty in 2012; and the pierced and painted wooden obelisks in the reconstructed Elizabethan garden at Kenilworth Castle, opened in 2008 (page 15).

The Gregory family
Coventry 1933

Design: City Engineer's Department
Size: Small
Material: Coventry Sandstone
Location: Open space by Stivichall Croft CV3
Bus: 9/9A to Stivichall Croft or X17 or 18A to Kenilworth Road or Park & Ride South to terminus
Nearest rail station: Coventry
Parking: Small car parks in Coat of Arms Bridge Road; walk 150 metres beyond bridge

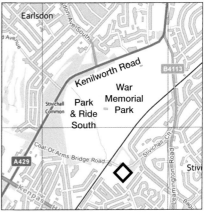

Map contains Ordnance Survey Data © Crown copyright and database 2011, 2012.

The Gregory family acquired property in Coventry, Stivichall (pronounced stye-chul) and Kingshill from the sixteenth century. They built Stivichall Hall 1750-60.

By the 1920s Coventry had become a manufacturing centre for motor cars, motorcycles, bicycles and aircraft. Its population was increasing; enterprise was expanding. People recognized that the city needed more room for houses, factories, roads, sewage works and an aerodrome. The Corporation secured Acts of Parliament to extend the city's boundaries, first in 1927 and again in 1931. Ambitious town planning proposals were published in 1932.

Despite developments elsewhere, the parish of Stivichall remained, by a happy chance, untouched by urbanisation. There was widespread regret when the Gregory family started to build houses on their land from 1928. A Stivichall Preservation Scheme was instituted, perhaps at the prompting of the Town Clerk, to protect Stivichall Hamlet from twentieth-century intrusions. It was a picturesque spot which, adjacent to Stivichall Common, was a popular walk for Coventry people. There were cottages around a tree-shaded green with an old pinfold; there was a smithy and a pond. One of the cottagers, Mrs Sparrow, served teas.

The Corporation bought nine and a half acres in 1929. Then in 1932, with their encouragement, Major Gregory-Hood made a gift of one and a quarter acres to complete a scene that evoked bygone Warwickshire. The gift came with some substantial conditions, one of them requiring the Corporation to erect a stone in the hamlet recording the gift and commemorating the Gregory family. Stivichall Hamlet presented a mixed picture: the City Engineer had the cottages painted up while dead elms remained on the village green. Then in the winter of 1932-33 the red sandstone obelisk was made and installed by Messrs J.H. Taylor of Coventry for the tender price of £75. The bronze tablet was produced by Messrs Stilwells of Coventry at a cost of £12 7s 6d. The appearance of 'A Stivichall Memorial' was noted by the *Coventry Herald*, February 17 & 18, 1933. At about the same time the Stivichall obelisk became the model for the memorial to the Conservators of the Stoke Commons.

An article in *The Guildsman* concocted a word-picture of the walk to Stivichall Hamlet as it was then in 1969. It lamented the danger of traffic, the general neglect, the loss of atmosphere and human interest; the hamlet presented a "sad and woebegone picture". Today a hedgerow separates the obelisk from the former village green, now known as Chideock Hill open space.

LEFT: *The obelisk and the former blacksmith's house and forge.*
BELOW: *The Forge.*
PHOTO: Coventry History Centre

The obelisk stands by Stivichall Croft. A tablet records:

THIS GREEN
WITH THE ADJOINING HAMLET
OF STIVICHALL
WAS PRESENTED TO THE CITY
OF COVENTRY
IN 1932
BY MAJOR CHARLES HUGH
GREGORY-HOOD
IN MEMORY OF THE GREGORY
FAMILY
WHO WERE OWNERS OF THE
MANOR OF STIVICHALL
FOR OVER 400 YEARS

A nineteenth-century view of Stivichall hamlet with a train crossing the Coat of Arms Bridge in the background. Opened in December 1844, the railway was a massive intrusion. The old pinfold or pound is on the west side of it.
© Coventry History Centre

20 The Conservators of the Stoke Commons

Coventry 1933

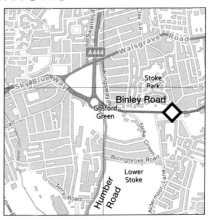

Design: City Engineer's Department
Size: Small
Material: Coventry Sandstone
Location: Open space at the junction of Bray's Lane with Binley Road, Stoke, Coventry CV2
Bus: National Express 13, 13A from city centre
Nearest rail station: Coventry
Parking: Supermarket or side streets, considerately

Map contains Ordnance Survey Data © Crown copyright and database 2011, 2012.

In the mediaeval period Coventry people had rights of common, that is, they could graze cattle and horses on the extensive areas of Lammas lands, Michaelmas lands and waste surrounding the city. (Lammas Day, 1st August, marked the end of haymaking; Michaelmas, 29th September, marked the end of the harvest; waste was unused or uncultivated land). By the nineteenth century the waste included Stoke Heath, Stoke Aldermoor, and stretches of land on either side of Binley Road including Gosford Green, Stoke Green and Stoke Hill.

Rights of common had been granted from at least the time of Godiva when much of the land was woodland. Over the centuries, as elsewhere in Arden, it was cleared piecemeal by individuals and institutions for grazing, fuel or crops. Steadily, pieces of land were enclosed or encroached upon, sometimes with the sanction of the Corporation, sometimes not. From the 15th to the 17th centuries particularly, enclosure was violently resisted, even reversed, by angry townspeople. There was hostility to private landowners especially when they abused commoners' rights by, for example, obstructing access or by growing crops on grazing land.

The management of the common lands was vested in two chamberlains. They inspected boundaries, organised the collection of stray animals by the pinners or pinders, and reported abuses and infringements. By the mid-nineteenth century the chamberlains had no other important functions, and only a small minority of freemen exercised their rights of common. They, however, developed as vigorous a resistance to enclosure as in previous centuries.

The obelisk is in public open space beside the Binley Road. The main inscription reads:

THIS MEMORIAL COMMEMORATES THE WORK DONE ON BEHALF OF THE PARISH AND PEOPLE OF STOKE BY THE CONSERVATORS OF THE ANCIENT COMMONS OF THE PARISH. THE CONSERVATORS WERE IN CONTROL OF THE COMMONS FROM 1889 TO 1928, WHEN THEIR DUTIES WERE TAKEN OVER BY THE CORPORATION OF COVENTRY.

A second plaque records the names of the conservators who were in office in 1928.

ABOVE: *Aerial view of Stoke and its open spaces; north is to the top.* Coventry History Centre

ABOVE: *Stoke Heath with Stoke Common on the right.*
Coventry History Centre

LEFT: *A summer's evening, Stoke Park, formerly Stoke Common.*

"The freemens' resistance was to have serious effects on the development of Coventry. In a letter to the Corporation of 1843 the secretary of the Health of Towns Commission stressed the unnatural check to the ordered growth of the town resulting from its encircling belt of commons. New building was, at this date, crowded within the old town to the detriment of public health. At the same time the conditions of tenure hindered the development of market-gardening to feed the new population adequately." Also, new uses created requirements for land that were sanctioned by Acts of Parliament: for railways, turnpikes, and the London Road Cemetery, resulting in losses of common land.

By 1860 a majority of freemen were in favour of enclosure and were compensated in land, but the compensation estate was gradually reduced by sales and requisitions for industry and housing. In a second enclosure of 1875 the rights of pasture were shared between the Corporation and the freemen but by 1894 the freemen had sold their portion and invested the proceeds – the pattern for future disposals.

The remaining wastes and commons continued in use as pasture but the need for more recreation grounds made inroads into the wastes. "Arrangements made for the management of Stoke Common in 1886 specifically reserved to the inhabitants the privilege of playing cricket and other games there, although grazing was still allowed. In 1841 the common land in Stoke covered 75 acres." From 1886 to 1927 the pasture and general administration of Stoke Common was vested in a body of conservators. Nevertheless, in 1916 a warworkers' housing estate of more than 800 houses was built on Stoke Heath. Gosford Green was reserved for recreational purposes by the corporation in 1914 in return for an annual payment to the freemen's trustees set up in 1860.

The Coventry Corporation Act of 1927 extinguished all the remaining traditional rights of common within the city boundaries. By then the remainder of Stoke Green, Stoke Heath and Stoke Hill comprised just over 58 acres; their legal status was changed and they became public open spaces along with the other remaining wastes, with compensation paid to the freemen's trustees. "Hence, although there are several areas of land in Coventry which are popularly known as 'commons', none in fact now have that legal status. Those which belonged to the manor of Coventry were Hearsall, Radford and Whitley commons, and those which belonged to the manor of Stoke are Barras Green, Stoke Green and Stoke Heath."

In December 1932, around the time that the memorial to the Gregory family, Lords of the Manor of Stivichall, was being installed, the corporation approved the suggestion by Councillor Malcolm that "for historical reasons" a memorial be erected to the late conservators of the Stoke Commons. The City Engineer's design, which closely resembled the obelisk at Stivichall (page 63), together with the inscriptions, were approved in June 1933. Whether intentionally or not, the two nearly identical obelisks represent age-old antagonists, commoners and landowners. The obelisk was erected in 1933.

New obelisks in public places

Obelisk at the Armed Forces Memorial, National Memorial Arboretum, Alrewas, Staffordshire.
PHOTO: Brian Chadwick / geograph.org.uk

Memorial unveiled in 2012 to six airmen of 9 EFTS, Ansty Aerodrome, who died over Ansty during World War II.
PHOTO: Peter Warrilow

A general war memorial at St Mary's Church, Pype Hayes, Birmingham.

Pyramidal obelisk near Edgehill, part of the Ratley Millennium Element Trail and reminiscent of Compton Pike, the sixteenth-century pyramidal beacon near Compton Wynyates.

Further information

WCRO: Warwickshire County Record Office.
WGT: Warwickshire Gardens Trust.

GENERAL & BACKGROUND

Barnes, Richard. *The obelisk: a monumental feature in Britain.* Norfolk, Frontier Publishing, 2004.

Coffin, David R. *The English Garden: meditation and memorial.* Princeton University Press, 1994.

Curl, James Stevens. *The art and architecture of freemasonry.* London, Batsford, 1991.

Curl, James Stevens. *Egyptomania: The Egyptian revival: a recurring theme in the history of taste.* Manchester University Press, 1994.

McGrory, David. *The Illustrated History of Coventry's Suburbs.* Derby, Breedon Books, 2003.

Mowl, T. and James, D. *Historic Gardens of Warwickshire.* Bristol, Redcliffe Press Ltd, 2011.

Noszlopy, George T.
Public sculpture of Warwickshire, Coventry and Solihull. Liverpool University Press, 2003.
Public sculpture of Birmingham, including Sutton Coldfield. Liverpool University Press, 1998.

EGYPT AND ROME

Dibner, Bern. *Moving the obelisks.* Norwalk, Conn., Burndy Library, 1991, 4th edition.

Habachi, Labib. *The obelisks of Egypt: skyscrapers of the past.* London, J M Dent & Sons, 1978.

1. KENILWORTH CASTLE

Martyn, Trea. *Elizabeth in the garden.* Faber & Faber, 2008.

Woodhouse, Elizabeth. *Kenilworth, the Earl of Leicester's pleasure grounds following Robert Laneham's letter.* Garden History Journal, Summer 1999, pp.127-144.

Woodhouse, Elizabeth. *Propaganda in Paradise: the symbolic garden created by the Earl of Leicester at Kenilworth.* Garden History Journal, Spring 2008, pp.94-113.

Strong, Roy C. *Federigo Zuccaro's visit to England in 1575.* Warburg Journal 1959.

2. FARNBOROUGH

National Trust guides, 1978 & 1984.

3. UMBERSLADE

Cousins, Mike. *The Umberslade obelisk.* Follies Magazine, Spring 2006.

Pettinger, John W. *Tanworth in Arden.* Brewin Books, 2005.

CEMETERIES

Birmingham City Council Bereavement Services information leaflets for Brandwood
    End, Lodge Hill, South Yardley and Witton cemeteries (downloadable from
    www.birmingham.gov.uk)

Curl, James Stevens. *A celebration of death.* London, Constable, 1980.

Curl, James Stevens. *The Victorian celebration of death.* Stroud, Sutton Publishing
    Limited, 2004.

English Heritage. *Register of Parks and Gardens of Special Historic Interest: Witton
    Cemetery, Birmingham.*

Lovie, Jonathan. *Key Hill Cemetery and Warstone Lane Cemetery, Birmingham.* WGT,
    2001.

Lovie, Jonathan. *London Road Cemetery, Coventry.* WGT, 2001.

4. COMPTON VERNEY

Bearman, Robert, ed. *Compton Verney: a history of the house and its owners.* Shakespeare
    Birthplace Trust, 2000.

Claydon House. Verney Papers 10/961/26. Undated letter, Lord Henry to his wife's niece.

Keast, John. *The King of Mid-Cornwall: Life of Joseph Thomas Treffry 1782-1850.* 1982.

5. FIENNES MILLER, Edgehill

National Army Museum 6807-244. Copies of letters to Lt-Col Fiennes Miller.

The Marquess of Anglesey FSA. *A history of the British cavalry 1816-1919,* Vol.1:
    1816-1850. Prologue (iv) The Waterloo campaign, 1815.

Jackson, Major E S. *The Inniskilling Dragoons: the records of an old heavy cavalry
    regiment,* from p.137 The Waterloo campaign. London, Arthur L Humphreys, 1909.

6. HOO HILL, Polesworth

The National Archives. Records and plans of the Trent Valley Railway.

WCRO. DR(B)44/110. Polesworth parish records.

WCRO. DR(B)20/13. Polesworth Vicarial Register [a scrapbook in a blank register].

WCRO. Minutes of Atherstone Rural District Council.

Warwickshire County Council Minutes.

7. THOMAS UNETT, Birmingham

Chinn, Carl. *Remember the Crimean War's valiant colonel.* Birmingham Mail, 28
    January 2006.

Staffordshire Record Office. D3610/16/1. Lt-Col.T Unett, Crimean Journal, April
    1854-March 1855; D3610/16/2. Sketchbook.

8. WILLIAM CHESHIRE, Stratford-upon-Avon

Inscriptions transcribed from the front and back of the obelisk itself.

9. EDWARD WILLES, Leamington

WCRO. CR 934. Memoranda book of William Willes 1873-1881.

WCRO. CR 1538/18. Jephson Gardens Trustees minutes from 1858.

WCRO. CR 1538/19-21 1851-80. Jephson Gardens Management Committee
  minutes.

10. THE PHILIPS FAMILY, Welcombe Bank

Lovie, Jonathan. *W. A. Nesfield 1794-1881 Welcombe Hotel*. WGT, 1994.

Tyack, Geoffrey. *Warwickshire Country Houses*. Phillimore 1994.

11. HENRY BUCK, Birmingham

Birmingham Daily Post. Birmingham Archives and Heritage.

19th Century British Library Newspapers online via Birmingham Library.

www.oddfellows.co.uk: History of the Oddfellows.

Wikipedia articles: Friendly Societies; Odd Fellows; Oddfellows.

12. HENRY BRIGHT, Leamington

Dudley, T.B. *A complete history of Royal Leamington Spa*. Leamington, 1901.

Hobbs, Chris. *Horatio Bright c1828-1906*. www.chrishobbs.com/horatiobright.htm

Kadish, Sharman. *Jewish Heritage in England: an architectural guide*. English Heritage,
  2006.

Seaby, Wilfred A. *Clockmakers of Warwick and Leamington (to 1850)*. Warwickshire
  Museum, 1981.

13. FROM NEW STREET TO WITTON, Birmingham

Catherine Hutton Beale. *Memorials of the Old Meeting House and Burial Ground,
  Birmingham*. 1882.

Richard Foster. *Birmingham New Street, the story of a great station*, vols 1 & 2. Didcot:
  Wild Swan Publications Ltd., 1990.

14. BURNABY OF THE BLUES, Birmingham

Birmingham Archives and Heritage. Newspaper reports.

Burnaby, F.G. *A Ride to Khiva*. 1876.

Dictionary of National Biography, Oxford, 2004.

WAR MEMORIALS

Boorman, D. *At the going down of the sun: British First World War memorials*. York, W
  Sessions 1998.

Borg, Alan. *War memorials from antiquity to the present*. Leo Cooper, 1991.

The Imperial War Museum maintains the United Kingdom National Inventory of War
  Memorials, online at www.ukniwm.org.uk

The names of the fallen may also be recorded in a *Roll of Honour*. Many have been published for regiments, places, force and conflict. They are usually held by local public libraries.

15. RADFORD, Coventry

Coventry City Council, Leisure and Recreation Committee, 31 March 1981, section 2, minute 166.

Coventry History Centre. *Coventry Evening Telegraph.* 1981, April 9, p.28.

Coventry History Centre. *Coventry Herald* and *Coventry Standard.* 1919, December 26 & 27.

Coventry History Centre. *Coventry Standard.* 1945-1950, November.

Richardson, Kenneth. *Twentieth-Century Coventry.* London, Macmillan, 1972.

16. CYCLISTS, Meriden

Coventry History Centre. *Coventry Standard* and *Coventry Herald.* 1921, May 27 & 28.

Haythornethwaite. *A Photohistory of World War One.* London, Arms & Armour Press, 1995.

North Birmingham Cyclists' Touring Club. *Northern News.* Number 141, November 2005.

Resources for Learning in Scotland. *Pathfinder Pack on Bicycling - History* www.rls.org.uk

Warwick Library. *Warwick & Warwickshire Advertiser,* 1921, May 21 and 28.

17. THE 29TH DIVISION, Stretton on Dunsmore

Holland, Chris and Jordan, Tony. *The story behind the monument: the 29th Division in Warwickshire and north Oxfordshire, January-March 1915.* Stretton Millennium History Group, 2005.

Moorehead, A. *Gallipoli.* London: André Deutsch Ltd, 1989.

Warwick Library. *Warwick & Warwickshire Advertiser,* 1921, May 28.

Warwickshire Gardens Trust. *Dunsmore Heath Avenue.* Newsletter, Spring 1996.

18. SHUCKBURGH WAR MEMORIAL, Lower Shuckburgh

Rugby Library. *Rugby Advertiser,* 1921, November 25.

19. THE GREGORY FAMILY, Coventry

Bearman, Robert. *The Gregorys of Stivichall in the Sixteenth Century.* Coventry & Warwickshire History Pamphlets: No.8. Coventry Branch of the Historical Association, 1972.

20. THE CONSERVATORS OF THE STOKE COMMONS, Coventry

The City of Coventry, the common lands *in* Victoria County History. Warwickshire, Volume 8.

City of Coventry, Baths and Parks Committee, Minute Book No.6, 1931-36.

Smith, F. *Six Hundred Years of Municipal Life.* Coventry: Corporation of the City of Coventry, 1945.

Credits

The Warwickshire Gardens Trust would like to thank the following people and organisations for valuable information and advice: Caroline Beddall, Sue Collins, Norma Hampson, Jennifer Meir, Ben Morton, Sylvia Pinches, Malcolm Stirling, the staff and collections of Birmingham Archives and Heritage; Birmingham City Council Bereavement Services; the Coal Authority; Coventry History Centre at the Herbert Art Gallery and Museum; The National Archives; National Army Museum; Shakespeare Birthplace Trust Records Office; Staffordshire County Library, Tamworth; Staffordshire County Record Office; Warwickshire County Record Office; Warwickshire County Libraries at Atherstone, Leamington, Nuneaton, Polesworth, Rugby, Stratford-upon-Avon and Warwick. Photographs are credited where they appear; others are by Robin Stott. Every effort has been made to obtain permission to reproduce other photographs. Map extracts: Ordnance Survey OpenData VectorMap District. Group members were Jean Nicholson (drawings, county map base and photos), Shirley Stirling (text and background information), Robin Stott (photos, text and editing) and Peter Warrilow (photos, support and oversight). Special thanks go to Shirley Stirling for kindly hosting the group's meetings.

Looking at Warwickshire's obelisks were LEFT TO RIGHT: *Jean at Farnborough, Shirley at Napton, Robin at Dunchurch.* PHOTO: Jean Nicholson, *Peter and Burnaby, Birmingham.*

Warwickshire Gardens Trust

The Trust was formed in 1991. It is one of the 36 county gardens trusts in England.

We welcome new members. Join us for an enjoyable programme of talks and visits. The website has a list of the Trust's many publications as well as the year's programme and a downloadable membership application form.

Website: www.warwickshiregardenstrust.org.uk
Email: membership@warwickshiregardenstrust.org.uk

The Association of Gardens Trusts website has details of gardens trusts in other counties: www.gardenstrusts.org.uk

These be not obelisks

Each has been called an obelisk and each has its own story.

CLOCKWISE FROM TOP LEFT:
Long Compton War Memorial
Scouts War Memorial, Cannon Hill Park, Birmingham
George Eliot Memorial, Nuneaton
Column and sundial, Alscot Park
Milepost over market cross, Dunchurch
PHOTO: Jean Nicholson

Index

Pooley Hall Colliery
Tamworth
Polesworth
Hoo Hill 6
Walsall
Baddesley Ensor
Sutton Coldfield
Hurley
Hinckley
Nuneaton Colliery
Witton 13
Nuneaton
Pype Hayes
7 11 14 BIRMINGHAM
St Philip's Churchyard
Exhall
Meriden 16
Radford 15
Ansty
COVENTRY Triumph & Gloria
Church Lawford
Gregory 19 20 Stoke
Rugby
Hockley Heath
17 29th Division
Kenilworth 1
Umberslade 3
Rowington
Redditch
9 12 LEAMINGTON
Beaudesert
Warwick
St Mary's
Shuckburgh 18
Whitnash
Napton on the Hill
Welcombe Bank 10
Priors Hardwick
STRATFORD
Compton
Verney 4
Wormleighton
William Cheshire 8
Farnborough 2
Edgehill 5
Evesham
Ratley
Banbury
Shipston
Sutton under Brailes

Warwickshire, the historic county

Featured obelisks 1-20
Other obelisks ◆ (mostly war memorials)